ASTRAL PROJECTION

The Out-of-Body Experience Extremely Simplified

Zainurrahman

F&Z Publishing

2020

F&Z Publishing

https://fzpublishingstore.wordpress.com

fzpublishingstore@gmail.com

Indonesia

First Published 2020

ISBN-13: 979-8637381883

To my sons:

Death is nothing but illusion (~Dad)

Table of Contents

PREFACE

I am interested in the experience of astral projection for a long time but only this time I had the opportunity to write about that very interesting topic. In recent years, I have been preoccupied with a variety of psychokinesis topics and the subconscious mind. As a result, several books on telekinesis, clairvoyance, as well as mind control have been successfully written and have helped many people; at least they admit it.

This time I make every effort to explain the experience of astral projection and how you can experience it. In this case, I'm not just a writer but also someone who has projection experience. When I started writing this book, I didn't know where to start. I then read some popular books about astral projection to find a starting point.

I find that these books are certainly useful but on the one hand, are very theoretical. The book written by Sylvan Muldoon (*The Projection of the Astral Body*) is more impressed like a storybook with explanations that for me are not systematic. I then read the book *Astral Dynamics* written by Robert Bruce. This book, in my opinion, is better than Muldoon's. Muldoon makes no difference between etheric projections and astral projections. Muldoon explained the etheric projection using the term astral. However, Bruce also uses too many complicated concepts in his book. I believe that people need a simpler astral projection guide. I then focused on Brennan's book (*The Astral Projection Workbook*). When I read Brennan's book, I almost canceled my intention to write a book on astral projection. Unfortunately, the occult impressions are too thick in his book. Meanwhile, astral projections should be explained as natural and easy to experience. I was determined to write this book.

If you think this book is too short, it's because there isn't much to explain about this astral projection. Nevertheless, I admit that simplifying the experience of astral projection is not easy, even though I did it. You can prove it yourself.

Through this book, you will be guided to make various preparations so that you are qualified to experience astral projection. I also wrote a few things that could potentially frustrate the experience of astral projection. I have not found these things in other astral projection books.

I thank you for finding this book because, without you, my efforts will be in vain. Writing this book requires hard work and experiments that are literally "dangerous". I confirm one thing for you. Although you really want to experience conscious astral projection, if you have health problems especially those related to the heart, then never try astral projection. And finally, if I can ask for your help, constructive commentary on this book is very useful.

Part One

Basic Understanding

"If the scientists believed that the afterlife is the dimension of consciousness, they must be a step further."

UNDERSTANDING ASTRAL

The term *astral* was originally used by Plato in his description of another dimension among the stars he called *celestial spheres*. Etymologically, that word was a derivation of Latin *Astrum* (or *Astron* in Greek) that meant *stars* as a noun. Today, the term *astral* can be found in *astronomy* or *astrology* which is closely related to the stars, galaxy, or planets. In the context of astral traveling aka astral projection, the term *astral* should not be understood as a "trip across the planets and stars." The term *astral* in this context should be understood as a metaphorical adjective that means *higher*. For example, the term *astral plane* refers to a "higher plane"; higher from this earthly plane called a *physical plane* that has been associated for a long time to the earth.

Merriam Webster Dictionary, as I believe as a responsible dictionary, terminologically defines *astral* as anything that involves the spirit or the soul rather than the body. I had an assumption that the term *astral plane* could be "simplified" to "spiritual plane" or "the world of spirits" until my experience taught me that they are different planes. Although it is true – that the astral plane is the spiritual plane alone, that simplification seems to not simplify anything for the *spirit* itself is still "mysterious" for the rest of us, no matter how many theories exist over the books. Moreover, the spiritual discussions are best referred to the pages of the Holy Books and for some reason, those are often considered mythical; though, it is not one hundred percent true that those are mythical.

Many astral traveling books (if not all) discussed the meaning of astral. It is said that the astral plane is the next closest of the unseen plane to the physical plane. Even, it is also said that the astral plane is further divided into seven sub-planes. These theoretical explanations of the astral plane, or astral in general, is, at least for some people like me, complicated or too much. It's not that I could not digest the ideas. I just found that the astral and astral plane should not be that complicated.

Astral traveling, for example, is always "easy" if we see that as an experience. Most of the astral travelers or "projectors" even knew nothing about their astral traveling experiences or OBE (out-of-body experience). When we try to look at the esoteric or mystical explanation about that particular experience, we deal with at least two "difficulties". The first one is there are so many technical terms and explanations that not all people simply cannot grasp. The second one is not all people stand on the same path, belief system. When astral traveling is discussed, either orally or written, by mystics or esotericists, it sounds like an occult practice while no all people are interested in occultism.

Many people rely on scientific explanation and proof. The scientists are expected to make us understand the astral dynamics. Nonetheless, no matter how many projectors' name mentioned by the authors of astral projection to make their claims solid (that astral projection is a real thing), there is no scientific evidence that there is a consciousness or soul which is separated from normal neural activity or that one can consciously and literally leave the body and make an observation. For that reason, many scientists categorized astral traveling under pseudoscience.

In other words, the scientists believed that the phenomenon where someone feels (as if) he leaves his body and makes observation exists. However, they also believed that it has nothing to do with the soul or spirit. It is a product of particular neurological processes occurring in the brain. For instance, the fMRI scan showed them that when someone is experiencing anything they call astral traveling or OBE in general, there is a strong deactivation of the visual cortex while several areas associated with kinesthetic imagery are significantly activated.

Moreover, what the scientists know about this is that astral traveling can be induced by many factors like brain traumas, sensory deprivation, near-death experience (NDE), dissociative and psychedelic drugs (including certain mushrooms or cannabis), dehydration, sleep, and electrical stimulation of the brain. My personal experience even taught me that astral traveling can be induced by hypnotism.

It is not surprising that between sciences and mystics (including esotericism, occultism, and even religious belief), there is a wide gap in almost anything. Certainly, for science, there is no such thing called the astral. The sciences of consciousness (psychology and neurology) believe that there is only mind or consciousness.

I used to think that both science and mysticism just used different terms to refer to the same thing. For example, the psychology that came from the root *psyche* which means *soul*. I am aware that from the first time psychology was not intended to study about the soul or spirit (like in mystical concept) but I am afraid if it was the same thing. As psychology developed as a discipline with scientific methods, anything related to soul and spirit has fallen outside its domain. Therefore, for the psychologists, for example, the soul is the mind itself. The term *mind* for psychologists is more than how it is understood by the majority. When they use that term (mind), it does not always mean that they have discovered everything about it. The mind alone is still a "mystery" until today. A note to take: for some other people, the soul is not the mind alone. The soul is a conduit for the soul to express itself.

I was lucky to have a chance to read scientific papers about astral projection and books written by considerable writers about it. I found a few "new agers" book about astral traveling too. As a hypnotherapist, I also have some experience in inducing astral traveling with my clients with surprising results. From all the literature that I read, I found that the techniques are similar with a few modifications here and there. All techniques require certain works with the body and mind. I then persuaded myself to not looking at the differences but the similarities. The key to understanding the astral dynamics (astral plane, astral traveling, etc.) is to pour into a bowl what all literature said about it.

The terms and explanations are certainly different. Mystics had their astral experiences and the scientists had their investigation reports. They had their experiences but they described those experiences differently. Nevertheless, it was the same experience; the same experience described in different words and manner.

I am neither a mystic nor a scientist. However, I have OBE experiences and successfully made other people experience it too. As I told before that I am a hypnotherapist, I studied self-hypnosis and I am fully aware that self-hypnosis is a great tool to experience an OBE. Also, because of one or other reasons, I practiced psychokinesis which brought me into meditation. During deep meditativeness, OBE happened as well. I am also a firm religious believer and those OBE experiences I had confirmed my religious belief that the other dimensions (afterlife) exist. I had carefully tested and contemplated various techniques prescribed by mystics and science and I concluded that they were all talking or teaching the same thing. The perspectives and vocabularies blurred the big picture.

Allow me to involve a brief religious discussion in this part. Almost all religions (if not all) and mystical beliefs teach us that we are all more than a body. Scientifically, the mind, and furthermore the consciousness, is beyond the body. Certainly, mystics and sciences have different perspectives in looking at consciousness. Some scientists believed that consciousness is the product of electrical impulses that occurred in the brain. However, there is an important question to raise here. If consciousness is nothing more than the product of electrical impulses in the brain, can we make a dead body turns conscious by stimulating electricity in that physical brain (by mimicking the natural electrical impulse in a living brain)? I think that we may make the body moves when the electricity strikes a certain part of the brain like the motor cortex. However, I believe that it will not make that dead body returns conscious. At this point, the mystics may have one point further than the scientists who believed that the consciousness is a brain product for they believe that the consciousness resides at its place, the multileveled dimension they called *planes* and one of the planes is the *astral plane*.

Even among the scientists themselves, consciousness is still a controversial topic. They who were interested in *quantum physics* believed that consciousness is not "trapped" in the brain or body. The other scientists, on the other hand, believe just the contrary. Only a few psychologists believed that the consciousness, especially the subconscious, is beyond the body. A common man like me assumed that the consciousness may be centered in the brain and associated with particular glands but it is not limited to the scalp. My practice in psychokinesis and other related psychic phenomena just confirmed that assumption at least for me personally.

As a man dies, his physical glands stop working but for mystics, it does not mean that his consciousness goes off. It shifts to the subtler level dimension that every mystics or religion have their own words for that. Mystics or esotericism called it an astral plane. In Islamic belief, it is called Barzakh. In Judaism it is called Yetzirah, and so on. Since sciences are not interested to study the afterlife for they don't believe that it exists, they surely had no word to refer to that dimension.

Astral Plane

If the scientists believed that the afterlife is the dimension of consciousness, they must be a step further. Simply, the astral plane is a plane or dimension that all spirits or consciousness will reside when people die. It is a plane between this physical plane (the scientific plane) and the spiritual plane (the religious plane). I do believe that the astral plane is a void in its origin just like the consciousness before the creative intelligence of the mind builds anything within it. In other words, the content of the astral plane is heavily dependent on what we have "encoded" in the mind, say, memories, expectations, fears, and so on. I am aware that this statement is weak at this point. I am expecting you to read along so that this statement makes sense.

If you had read or watched reports or stories from the projectors, you would know that they had different experiences in their astral traveling. You must be aware that two people could not meet in the astral plane although they did astral projection at the same time and place. Even if they made an appointment, what they meet was a "person" with the same shape; it was shaped by the creative power of the mind.

It is unquestionable that our mind is creative. The creative power of the mind resides in the subconscious mind associated with the right hemisphere in the physical brain. Nevertheless, we know that the brain is a lump of protein that can do nothing without the consciousness that makes it to life; a dead man still has a brain but a not-working brain. The void of the astral plane is soon altered into either a romantic scene or a terrible one. It depends on the creative power of the mind, the luggage of the mind, and the ability of the person to control his mind. The memories of what he had done or what he expects to do also shape the astral plane. In the religious sense, it is what we call sin and goodness.

The astral plane is located neither on the sky above nor in the earth below. All writers of astral projection including myself believe that the astral plane occupies the same space as this physical plane. The space in your room is both physical and astral. You can physically sense the space physically and at the same time, you are also conscious of that space. It is the "mode of being" that enables or disables us from experiencing the space. If I am conscious of my physicality, I am experiencing a physical plane. On the other hand, if I am conscious of my astral, I switch to another plane. Let's say, if I am conscious of my subtler body (astral body), I switch to the astral plane. The simplest way to look at this phenomenon (of the mode of being) is thinking about sleeping. Sleeping is a kind of "switching to another mode of being."

Can you tell where you were or what you were conscious of when you were sleeping? I bet you can't, so do I. According to science, neuro-psychology, sleeping is a phenomenon when our brain works at the lowest level called *delta*. It is said as an unconscious state; *a state when we are unconscious of everything* but I prefer to say it *a state when we are conscious of nothing*. However, it does not tell where we are, right? Fortunately, we got the answer from a Holy Book, one of the references that the scientists would not refer to. The Holy Koran, the Holy Book of Muslims, the 42nd verse of the 39th surah, it says:

> "God is who taketh away souls at the time of their death, and those which die not in their sleep; then He withholds those on which He hath decreed death, and sendeth back the rest for an appointed term. Verily, herein are signs for a people who ponder (Holy Koran, 39:42)."

While we don't intend to discuss God or where He is, the verse suggests that during sleep our consciousness (remember that science puts spirit or soul and consciousness as equals) is in the other plane or dimension; it is not in the body or physical plane. We almost know nothing about where we are during sleep because that plane has nothing to associate with within the physical plane. Whereas, our mind has been – for a long time – habituated to associate anything with any other thing in the physical plane for we believe (or were taught to believe) that this physical plane is the only plane. We can paraphrase the statement to sound like this: the astral plane is a void where we are when we die or sleep.

The first basic principle for astral traveling to occur is to let the body asleep while the mind awakes or conscious. If we do this, we will fall into lucid dreaming first and then astral projection, unless we are deep sleepers. This is good information for you that lucid dreaming is a well-known and best doorway to astral projection. Even, for some projectors and writers, astral projection is an extremely heightened lucid dream.

The delta state or sleep is a state when the brain does not process the sensory stimuli as much as when we are awake. We are aware of the things around us because we can physically sense them. In other words, our consciousness in this physical plane relies on the physical sensory system. When we sleep, the brain does not process the information sent by the physical sensors so that the consciousness turns into the void of the astral plane and since we are not aware of nothingness, we are said to be unconscious.

In sleep, we dream. Freud said that we always have dreams during sleep but not all dreams are able to be remembered; only vivid dreams are remembered. Dreams are, according to Freud, the unconscious desires. In other words, dreams are desires repressed down into the unconscious mind. During sleep, our unconscious mind becomes conscious and the repressed contents are brought up. It is the lucidity that determines whether the dreams are remembered or recorded into the physical brain (to be memories) or not. Lucid dreaming or a controllable dream is an example of a dream with strong lucidity. The ability to control it depends on the level of awareness someone has. Do not confuse the lucid dream and astral projection. A lucid dream is a "playground" where we "play" the memories or unconscious desires, in the astral plane. The astral projection is the exploration of the "playground." Nonetheless, there is a reason why we call it "projection." It is a projection of the consciousness and anything it contains.

The astral plane is not a chaotic plane. It is a void. However, it is not a place where you cannot find anything. In fact, it is where pureness is found. In my own words, it is like a "kitchen" where all ingredients are there but no food. Well, you are the "cook".

There are many projectors who reported that they were walking among the buildings in the physical plane during astral travel. It is so because the astral plane occupies the same space as the physical plane. However, the nearest astral plane is not truly the astral plane but the *etheric plane*. When someone goes into the deep astral plane, he will not find the physical plane. Certainly, it is not an astral projection but an *etheric projection* if someone still finds the physical plane. His consciousness "drives" the *etheric body* aka *pranic body* or *energy body*. He walks within the energy field of the physical plane; the energy field emanated from the things in that physical plane. As he goes deeper, he enters the void. If he goes deeper than that, he enters the energy field of the "things" of the spiritual plane. What if he goes deeper and deeper? Does he enter the spiritual plane? I don't think so. He will enter the true spiritual plane when he dies, if we refer to the verse from the Holy Koran we quoted above.

In sum, the astral plane is the intermediate plane between the physical plane (body) and the spiritual plane (spirit). It is the plane of consciousness when we are not conscious of the physical plane for whatever reasons or causes. It is originally a void and the content is projected from the consciousness itself. How it behaves depends on the consciousness or the mind's creative power and the ability to control it. It does not mean that it is an imaginary plane. It is not created by imagination. Imagination itself exists within it, as I discuss in the other parts.

Switching to the Astral Plane

I have the worst words used to describe the switching to the astral plane: we always switch to the astral plane when our body and brain do not work "properly". Sleeping is one of them. The reason I said this is because our body and brain are supposed to be active agents to support our bodily existence. When we sleep, the brain works in its lowest state. The cortices decrease their works. Fortunately, the brain works that way for many good reasons. So, in this case, "not working properly" does not always mean something bad.

Nevertheless, the above words are metaphor as long as we refer to sleep or hypnosis. Astral projection has other triggers that treat the meaning of the above words literally, for example, physical illness, NDE, drugs, and brain traumas. Those are triggers of astral projection and those are conditions when the body and brain cannot function properly. If I am allowed to add one more trigger, it is death.

In many pieces of research on OBE, thousands of people reported that they experienced OBE like astral projection during surgery on the operation bed. This happened because they were either comma because of physical injuries or they were given total anesthesia so that they could not sense their body; their physical sensory systems didn't work so that their brain could not process the information sent by the physical sensory systems. The result, they became aware that they were aware of it. This awareness then filled their consciousness and being conscious of the non-physical awareness made them "free" from their physical body.

Drugs are also a considerable trigger to switch from the physical plane to the astral plane. However, many people could not experience astral travel with drugs or certain mushrooms just because they were too drunk to control it.

Fortunately, we don't have to get an NDE or drugs to experience astral travel. What we need to do is to dedicate our time to practice or to visit a responsible hypnotherapist to guide us to lower the brain activity and heighten the awareness on the other plane. In this part, let me give you a hint: sleep paralysis is a great way to astral projection if you are brave enough to experience it. Many people are afraid too much to sleep paralysis. Are you one of them?

Etheric and Astral Body

I was interested in psychokinesis, especially telekinesis, from 2017. Two years later, I wrote two books about it. The first book is a telekinesis practical guide for beginners (*Telekinesis: A Serious Guide*) and the second book is for them who want to develop their telekinesis skill (*Develop your Telekinesis Skill*). In 2019, I also wrote another psychic book about the ability to see with the mind's eye

(*Clairvoyance: A Serious Guide for Beginners*). Before and during the writing of those books, I practiced and did experiments with various techniques. Some techniques worked and some didn't work as I and everyone else might expect. I reached a conclusion that any techniques in "doing psychokinesis" work if they suit us. There is no universal technique that can work for all people. Nevertheless, one thing for sure, all people must understand that they have a subtler body right after the physical body. This body is made of *pure cosmic energy* known as *prana* or *chi* or *psi* or *ether*. This body is called *the etheric body* that the main function is to maintain the form and the stability of the physical body.

I had "seen" the fact that the etheric body is the intermediate between the physical body and the astral body or the *body of consciousness*. The etheric body is somehow still "physical" because it can be sensed with the physical body and it can bring particular effects to the physical object around the body. Telekinesis confirms that assumption. It can be "driven" by the consciousness to have particular visions in particular distances. Clairvoyance confirms that assumption.

The physical body can sense the etheric body as vibration or electromagnetic impulses that for many scientists is nothing but a *placebo effect*. I used to believe this perspective until I could make other people sense my etheric body (my energy) and I could move certain light objects without any physical contact and only by using that energy (directed by the mind intention). To do this, the etheric body must be cultivated and there are many systems of energy work that someone can pick to practice regularly. Yoga and Qigong are two of the systems to work with the etheric body.

It is said that the etheric body has its centers. In Yoga, those centers are called *chakras* and in Qigong, those are called *dantiens*. There are seven major chakras in Yoga and three of them are in Qigong. These systems are practiced (one of them or both) to realign, replenish, restore, and strengthen the etheric body.

The etheric body is an energy field that forms our physical body and sustains the form. It is said (by science) that all the cells in our body are regenerated within 6 months. It means that within 6 months we are physically a totally different person. If you meet a friend you didn't meet for 7 months, you actually meet a totally different body. However, you still recognize him because in your eyes nothing had changed significantly unless he went for plastic surgery. It is so because your friend's etheric body sustained his physical form like face structure.

The etheric body is sometimes referred to as *the pranic body* because it is made of *prana*. The term *prana* (in Hinduism) equals to Chi (in Chinese) or Ki (in Japanese). There is no exact English translation for those terms but a general English translation is *energy*. Because of its function to keep the physical body stable, it must be kept strong and healthy. In other words, it is "rechargeable".

The default recharging process takes place during sleep and eats (especially eating raw foods). Without being recharged, the etheric body turns weak and consequently, the physical body becomes weak too. This etheric body is also projectable and people who practiced *etheric projection* (that many people think astral projection) could make their etheric body exhausted. Without regularly recharging their etheric body, it is very possible that their physical body will suffer certain unexpected instabilities. We need to eat food and sleep well to recharge our etheric body for common daily activities also require the work of the etheric body.

The etheric body is always active and working. If it does not work properly, certain physical illnesses emerge. However, to practice etheric projection (consciousness travel within the physical plane), the etheric body must be cultivated. The etheric body is not supposed to "leave" the physical body because it is there to keep the physical body. Therefore, projection is additional work for it. This means that the etheric body cultivation does not imply the inactivity of the etheric body. Normally, the etheric body is not sensible until it is cultivated by practicing either yoga or qigong or else. It includes the enhancement of the physical sensitivity (kinesthetic sense) to "detect" the existence of the ether or prana.

The etheric body directly affects the physical body. You have heard anything about the mind-body connection, right? The mind is the astral body. The mind and the body are "bridged" by the etheric body. The mind or consciousness (they are not necessarily the same, of course) affects the etheric body and the etheric body affects the physical body. It is normally always like that. However, I had the experience that showed me if the etheric body could work without the physical body to react.

After almost two hours practicing telekinesis, I went to bed. The vibrating sensation on my hands' skin was still quite clear, especially in my palms and fingers. Usually, it took some minutes to fade but I think that night it took a little longer. On the bed, I laid my body on the left side. My left hand was pressed by my half-body and a pillow. It means that my left hand could not move freely. I was trying to relax my body and mind to get asleep faster because it was already late. After some minutes, suddenly, I felt my left hand vibrated smoothly and warm. I tried to feel my left hand and it became lighter as if it was not being pressed by anything. By using my intention and feeling, I moved my fingers slightly and I could feel it move. At the same time, I knew that my physical fingers didn't move. I moved my hand from fingers to elbow. It could move but just a little bit. Then, I squeezed my left hand physically and turned my body to the other side, to physically free my left hand. It was not easy to replicate the same thing to the other parts of my body. So, I decided to stop doing it. As time goes by, I felt my left hand was not aligned (the physical and the etheric). My left hand became weaker than usual until I did some exercises to realign it.

What I was experiencing is the etheric body. I regularly practice a qigong technique called Zhang Zhuang. In this practice, what I need to do is standing still in certain poses. During the standing position, I must focus on the etheric body. This is a simple practice that we can do to cultivate the etheric body. However, it is not always enjoyable. I used to think that moving practice is more enjoyable than standing or sitting still. It seems easy to do but hard to master. Then, I am aware that it is all about dedication. If you are interested in that practice, you can find the simplest guide in my telekinesis books.

The etheric body is the energy body that works with the physical body. However, don't imagine it like plastic wrapping meat. Imagine it like a light emitted from the bulb. The light is the energy and the bulb is the body. The etheric body is not a still body. It is a dynamic body that flows through the "lines" that in yoga is called *nadis* and in qigong is called *meridians*. It is miraculous that it flows from a part of the body to another part of the body without messing the body up. I mean, if it could not sustain its form, flowing from the head to toe may replace your head and toe position. It is like electricity. When it flows to a radio, it becomes sounds; if it flows to a television, it becomes sounds and pictures.

The etheric bodywork, if explained, is quite out of topic in this book. Therefore, let us skip the complexity. The most important thing is to be aware of the existence of the etheric body and what it does.

The etheric body can be "driven" by the consciousness or the mind. In clairvoyance, you can "load" the etheric body with your mind and then project it. It can merge with the other energy field and then unmerge so that you can pick information related to the object and receive it with your mind. Like in psychometry, what a clairvoyant does is that.

To work with the etheric body, you need to cultivate it (I know I already said it). Then, by relaxing the body and focusing on the breath (in and out), you will be aware of the electromagnetic impulses rush within your body and on your skin. It is the etheric body. When you shift your focus on certain parts of your body, you will feel the energy accumulated in that part. They move or flow. They have their default flow (direction) set by nature but your mind really can "change" the flow. It means that your mind alone can make the flow better. You can also mess up the flow and bring physical illness to your body just with your mind.

While the etheric body relates to the physical body, the astral body relates to the mind (or consciousness) that for mystics is soul or spirit. Right now, all the bodies are merged down into a particular structure to build "you." The etheric body makes sure that your physical body is stable and the astral body makes sure that you (as soul, spirit, consciousness) are in that physical body. They are all connected and consequently influencing each other. Your physical body can influence your mind and your mind can influence your body. Between the mind and the body are the astral and etheric bodies. They occupy the same space. Just like the universe; the astral plane (and the etheric plane, energy field, e.g. gravitation) occupies the same space as the physical plane (e.g. earth).

Now, let us turn to the astral body.

The astral body is the default plane for the consciousness; in etheric projection, the consciousness "drives" the etheric body. Originally, the astral body is responsible for mentality; although the etheric body, especially in the heart center, also influences emotion. The mind is in the astral body, certainly. You might have heard anything about the psychosomatic phenomenon. For example, anxiety (mental) can lead to ulcers. The anxiety is generated in the mind or emotion but people tend to repress or push it down to the etheric body (through the astral body). Since the etheric body manages the form of the physical body, the content (anxiety, which should not be there) influences the body.

The astral body is subtler than the etheric body. It makes the astral body is not physically sensible like the etheric body. However, the astral body can be experienced with the mind or consciousness or awareness. It has its apparatus substituting the physical sensory systems which are known as *astral senses*. With the astral senses, the consciousness can have visions without the physical eyes that work with the etheric body. You can smell a flower (physical, etheric) but you cannot smell a smell (astral, mind). You can see a house (physical, etheric) but you cannot see a vision (astral, mind). Through the astral senses, consciousness can have vision or others without the physical body. Your physical eyes (physical) receive light and its properties (density, color, size) and your brain converts it to electrical impulses in the brain (etheric) and send it to your mind-space (as sensations) and your mind-space (astral) throws it to the consciousness (you) so that you are aware of the color. All the sensations are "housed" in the astral body.

Let's return to the Holy Koran (39:42) for a while. That verse taught us that during sleep our astral body leaves the physical body. Is that the cause so that during sleep we cannot have any physical sensation? Is it because all the sensations reside in the astral body? Science will tell that during sleep our sensory systems keep sending signals to the brain but the brain does not process it as much as in the waking state. Is that about the brain or mind? All hypnotists know that guided imagery can lead the clients to local anesthesia, positive or negative hallucination, and so on. While the hypnotist does not "touch" the client's brain (even they don't have to touch the client's head), by using some special verbal suggestion, anesthesia is inducible. In this case, the sensation is related not only to the brain but also to the mind. The mind (astral) influences the brain (physical). Therefore, the Holy Koran and Science do not speak about a different thing; those speak the same thing in different "languages."

The astral body is the "house" of mind, consciousness, and anything related to it. However, it should not be seen as wrapping plastic. The astral body to the consciousness is just like the etheric body to the physical body. It makes sense now that either lucid dream or astral projection works with imagination as the trigger. For example, *The Rope Method*, a popular method of astral projection where the projector imagines climbing a rope to "exit" from his physical body, shows that the astral body works with the mind. This, of course, confirms the assumption.

The physical sensations might not be produced without physical senses; no input no output. However, as said, the astral body has its senses. In a lucid dream or ordinary dream, we see without the eyes open. How can we understand this?

Awareness and Astral Senses

Related to awareness, we know at least two ideas: *awareness* is the state of perceiving (ability to perceive) and knowing and the five physical senses are the main apparatus equipped to us *to be aware* of anything within a certain range. At this point, we want to distinguish "awareness" and "to be aware".

When we were kids, we were taught that it is the eyes that make us see, it is the nose that makes us smell, and so on. As knowledge develops by, we know that we can see because the visual cortex in the brain processes the impulses sent by the eyes and then send it to the mind-space and the mind interprets it as images. My son once asked me: why do some people sleep with their eyes half-open? I didn't know the answer. What I know is as long as the eyes open (although half-open), the light can enter and even when we sleep the brain still works although at its lowest level. But why their visual cortices don't process the light their eyes catch? In a worse example, for someone who is unfortunate and experiencing comma, his visual cortex cannot process the light sent by the eyes; if it processes the light, still he does not see anything. Should we assume that they (sleepers with eyes half open and the unfortunate one) don't see or they are simply unaware?

During sleep, all the physical sensory awareness is "disconnected" from consciousness. This state is what we know as *being unconscious*. It is so because of the astral body, as the house of the awareness, is "separated" from the physical body during sleep or in comma state. Reaching this point, I remember that we experience lucid dreaming and astral projection during sleep and many reported that they experienced astral projection (or etheric projection) in the operation bed (during surgery).

Now, if you close your eyes and block your ears with earplugs, you probably say that you cannot see and hear anything. For a reason, you are incorrect. If you are aware, the *darkness* and *silence* are there to be aware. Even if you block all the external inputs, you are still aware of where you are and what you are doing (the awareness is still there). Deep sleepers will fall asleep in seconds in that condition (blocked eyes and ears). Moreover, people who believe that awareness relies upon the physical sensory system will also fall asleep quickly. If they know that awareness is still there with them but has shifted to another environment, they will find it miraculous.

I am making a point that we don't deny that the physical senses are the main apparatus of physical awareness but those apparatus do not construct the awareness itself. Awareness is a faculty of information processing. If there is no information to process, the "processor" is still there. The awareness is still able to process the information from the other senses, the astral senses. The awareness is not tied to the physical senses but to the consciousness.

The term *astral sense* was popularized by occultism; any occultist believes that we do have astral senses connected to the astral body as the physical senses connected to the physical body. In Islamic esotericism, it is believed that the abilities to sense we have are lent by God. Without the eyes, we can see everything. The eyes are believed as the "blocks" that limit our vision to the physical plane. This physical body is believed to be a "prison of the soul" so that as long as we are living within this body, all sensations are limited to the physical sensation. Loosely translated, many people think that the astral body has eyes or ears. For example, the term *mind's eye* or *third eye* is believed to be the "eye of the soul." The pineal gland which is associated with the third eye is said to be the "seat of the soul." If it is the case, then the soul has only one eye; the soul is deaf because it has no ears (I know you've never heard the third ear because it does not exist even in concept). The most possible "shortcut" to solve this puzzle is to know that *awareness is the astral sense.*

If you search astral sense on the internet, your page will be loaded with too much information. I used to guide my client to imagine that she was speaking with her mother (RIP). She was under a deep hypnotic trance during this "mental conversation." When she woke up, she told me that she heard her mother's voice clearly. What happened to her was actually a "recalling" of the memories about her mother's voice. This showed me that if she was not aware of what she was doing (speaking with her mother in her imagination) she would not hear it. You may say that I didn't really know if she lied. That's fair enough. I also had my own experience. During an astral traveling, I heard voices, especially Holy Koran recitation. Not all astral projection experiences included auditory (or gustatory or olfactory) sensation but some of the experiences did.

It is possible that I made it by myself, by imagining it. Have you ever heard your name called when none was there? Many people experienced this whether they were sleeping, reading, watching TV, or cooking in the kitchen. Perhaps, it is their auditory cortex processing auditory memories but certainly, it is not a regular brain cortex activity because it does not happen every day. What about the clairvoyants who could see "thing" in a hundred miles distance and through times? What about the clairaudients who could hear "thing" beyond physical space and time? They could receive either "unusual" visual or auditory information while their eyes were widely open. They could do that either because they practiced it or they were indigos. My experiences taught me that what they did was turning their awareness from the external environment (physical) to the internal environment (astral). They "disconnected" their awareness from the physical senses and give priority to the astral plane which occupies the same space as the physical plane.

Let's have an experiment. Give yourself time to contemplate the darkness and silence especially when you are in your bed and attempting to sleep. As you close your eyes, your awareness may be still on the physical plane. That's why you feel as if you can see the corners of your bedroom and you can reach your cellphone although your eyes are closed. You don't see them with the third eye but you are aware of that situation. Usually, in this condition, we fill our minds with imagination expecting that we can fall asleep quickly. What you need to do is to be aware of the darkness surrounding you (because you close your eyes). Be fully aware that you are not seeing anything but the blackness. This is a kind of mindfulness practice. Pay attention to that blackness as long as you can. However, I know that you will, automatically, either return to the physical environment or turn into the astral environment, your awareness (you are aware that you are aware). The chance is the sounds around you (fan, AC, and so on) will go dim. If you pay attention to that sound or be aware of that sound, you will never turn into the internal environment. You will enter into a deeper state close to a sleep state called a *hypnagogic state*. In this state, images popup over your mind and you even cannot discriminate whether the images are physical or astral in that time. The only thing you know is that you are aware of it.

Make sure that your body is totally relaxed and you enjoy the experiment. If you fall asleep, it is not a mistake. The point is you are learning how to "turn inward" your awareness. If you "see" the vivid images, we don't call it "you see" but we call it "you have a vision." The faculty responsible for that vision is awareness which has turned inward. It applies to other information that you get (hearing, smelling, touching, etc.).

Now, let's go further to discuss what you experience during sleep; if you fall asleep. Since the astral plane is a void, what the astral senses (awareness) catch is the darkness and the silence. Perhaps, the word darkness is not appropriate here. I believe that the word *nothingness* is more representative. During sleep, we are aware of the nothingness and when we wake up we remember nothing. As long as the astral plane remains a void, the awareness catches nothing and this is often misunderstood as "being unaware" or "unconscious". It needs your ability to control awareness. It needs you to realize that you are the consciousness processing the awareness; while the awareness processes the inputs from physical senses.

You need to "build" the plane by utilizing the creative power of consciousness. You might read somewhere that the astral plane is inhabited by astral beings but for me, those being are projected from the consciousness. In the simplest words, how it looks like depends on the projection. I think this is the reason why we call it astral projection; it is all about projection. The astral plane is not a projection but how it looks like is. For example, if someone reported that he traveled to Mars and Moon during astral projection, he needed to see how Mars and Moon look like at least from YouTube. I mean, there is no Mars or Moon in the astral plane. Mars and moon are two physical entities in the physical plane. It is possible to travel to Mars without a physical body if you do etheric projection and not an astral projection.

Your creativity is required to build the things in the astral plane. This is the reason why it is not surprising that a *dream construct* is required in many astral projection techniques. I know that now astral projection sounds like lucid dreaming; many authors believe so. Unfortunately, a lucid dream is just a doorway to astral projection. Lucid dreaming is a dream. It occurs when you are asleep. Astral projection occurs between the edges of sleep and wakefulness. You can also lower down your travel to the etheric plane after successfully exit from your physical body so that you can walk around the real buildings in the physical plane. It is something that you cannot do in lucid dreaming.

THE ROLE OF BELIEF

The projection of the consciousness in different planes (astral plane, etheric plane) is real but the conscious experience of it is not available for all people, especially to people who disbelieve that it is real. I am not suggesting that astral projection is a belief-based experience. The point I am making is belief can either support or sabotage the experience.

We are talking about an item inhabiting the subconscious mind, *belief*. Let's first define what it is. Belief is any cognitive content held as true; while belief is *personal*, belief system represents the beliefs systematized in a group: religion, philosophy, teaching, etc.; it implies the "circle" of where someone belongs to.

To identify your belief is easy. Try to respond to this statement with **agree** or **disagree**: *astral projection is real*. What is your response? Many people may seek another option like *strongly agree* or *strongly disagree* that makes no difference. Some people expect that there is an option *I don't know* or *I doubt* that also makes no difference. There are only two options: agree or disagree.

Some people believed that astral projection is real but they always failed in consciously experiencing it. It is so because a belief has its sub-beliefs. You need to know what kinds of sub-beliefs potentially sabotage your attempts to experience astral projection. Here they are:

> *I believe that astral projection is real but I don't believe that I can experience it.*

> *I believe that astral projection is real and I believe I can experience it but I also believe that it is dangerous.*

> *I believe that astral projection is real, I can experience it, and it is safe, but I also believe that it is difficult.*

The beliefs after the "buts" are about to sabotage your attempts to have the miraculous experience of astral projection. So, you need to persuade your mind to change it to:

> *I believe that astral projection is real, I can experience it, it is safe, and it is easy.*

All the beliefs mentioned above are united and planted into a core-belief. It is what you believe about *what and who you are*.

I believe that changing a belief is not as easy as flipping the coin. Having experience as a hypnotherapist, I had a lot of experiences with the beliefs of the clients. Most of them had limiting beliefs in their head and those made them difficult to change or to develop. No matter how many experiences I had, I still believe that changing a belief is not an easy task. However, it is about changing someone's belief. If it is about changing my own belief, I know that I can believe whatever I want to believe. It applies to you too.

The following discussion is not an attempt to change your belief. Instead, it is a way for you to change your own belief if you want to experience astral projection. The fact that you are reading this book right now shows that you want to experience it. The rest will fall into place.

Now, let's turn to the core belief. What are you? The answer to this question is never personal. The answer is always within a system. I really don't know what your belief background about this. However, as long as I know, there are two big systems in the world: religious (religion-based, spirituality, spiritualism, mysticism, esotericism) and scientific (science, atheism) systems. You must be under one of these systems.

All systems mentioned above believe that human being is not a "single" element but a combination of two interconnected elements. In a religious belief system, a human being is a combination of body and spirit while in science (e.g. psychology) a human being is a combination of physic and mental. The simplest way to word these beliefs is "we are more than flesh."

The first and foremost factor for astral projection to happen is the "separation" between these two elements. This separation is only available if each element is originally independent; that the spirit or mental is an independent element that can be "freed" from the body or physic. Anyone who does not believe that spirit or mental is a separable element will never experience a conscious astral projection. Perhaps, they still have a chance to have that experience aided by drugs or particular mushrooms, or near-death experience (NDE). We don't really need all of those aids to experience astral projection, especially NDE.

The body and spirit, or the body and mental (mind), are interconnected. If they aren't, the body cannot be operated. See, the passive verb "operated" implies that there is an "operator." We are the operator of the body, say, spirit, mind, consciousness, and so on. The interconnectedness between the mind and the body is proven by the scientists through psychosomatic researches. Not only does the mind influence the body, but the body also influences the mind. People who practice yoga know that their bodily poses, positions, or movements are important to achieve targeted mental conditions (e.g. tranquility).

Did you find the answer to the question? That is what you believe; that is the core belief. That belief is either supporting or sabotaging your attempt to experience astral projection. How can? Belief is a part of the mind and it resides in the subconscious mind which according to Freud is far stronger (the effect to any physical and mental experience) than the conscious mind or the logical thinking mind.

Think about this. Astral projection experience requires the body to sleep while the mind awakes. It needs to work with the body and the mind to achieve this state. If you don't believe that you (as spirit, consciousness) are not separable from the physical body, then your belief will sabotage your attempt. Belief is a strong thought that can sabotage or support your attempt to have that miraculous experience. It does not mean that astral projection is mind-made. It is real. Your mind is just the power to make you achieve the experience or to block you from the experience. Most people failed because they had a "problem" with this core-belief; they had the belief that blocked them from the experience. Being failed to experience astral projection, their core-belief was strengthened and became stronger (that astral projection is not real).

PHYSICAL AND MENTAL CONDITIONING

To be honest, I don't have enough courage to say that astral projection is easy to be experienced consciously. Personally, based on experience, accidental astral projections are much easier compared to conscious and planned astral projections. Although I have quite a lot of experience with conscious astral projection, I also often have difficulty (even failing) in trying to have it. All of these experiences taught me that not only is the knowledge of astral projection is important but also the preparation of various aspects that allows the conscious astral projection to be experienced; if not well prepared, astral projection is either failed or, as explained later, "unrecorded".

Let us start by paying attention to the natural sleep that we experience every night. We know very well that in order to sleep, we need a calm mind and a relaxed body (we are talking about natural sleep without aids and drugs). Apart from the various theories about the astral projection that I and you have read before, I believe that astral projection is furtherance of sleep. Of course, I am not implying that astral projection is only a dream, but the astral projection is impossible if our conscious mind and body are still awake. Therefore, as with natural sleep, the astral projection also requires both physical and mental conditioning.

Without intending to create a fantastic impression through this book, I apply the division of preparation to astral projection in three parts; this is specifically applying to me and I just want to share with you. Perhaps, this is the simplest division you will ever find in books discussing astral projection. The first part is pre-projection (etheric body preparation); the second part is while-projection (physical relaxation, trance, doorway construction, and re-entry); the third part is post-projection (realignment). I hope you are not bothered by these terms and divisions. Eventually, you will understand that the key to astral projection is energy, trance, and consciousness.

Pre-Projection (etheric body preparation)

Please remember that this is the furtherance of working with the belief we discussed previously.

I understand that we had discussed the function of the etheric body and the difference between the etheric and astral projection. Someone may ask why it is important to prepare the etheric body if he is about to experience astral projection and not an etheric projection. That is a fair question and I want to address that question in this section.

The etheric body has something to do with the astral projection. Regarding astral projection, the etheric body plays at least two important roles. Firstly, the etheric body makes it possible for us to shift our awareness from the physical plane to the subtler plane, etheric and astral plane. Secondly, the etheric body is the conduit supplying energy to the astral body for "consciousness transfer" to occur and the astral body consciousness to be maintained. This conduit is the famous *silver cord* that you might have read in the other books.

We need to be reminded that the etheric body is the intermediary body between the physical body and the astral body. The astral body, during natural sleep, is "unconscious" or works automatically as the counterpart of the physical body. For example, as you are reading this book, your astral body automatically processes the sensations that are mostly ignored by your conscious mind. During natural sleep, the awareness of sensation is "off" or "we are sensing nothing" and "being aware of nothing". We are more aware of the physicality than astral. This awareness or consciousness must be transferred (or shifted) to the astral body so that the astral body can become "conscious". This is what we call conscious astral projection. The transference of consciousness starts when we shift it from the physical body to the etheric body. Semi-automatically, it will reach the astral body. In other words, it is difficult (if not impossible) to be aware of the awareness if we don't start to be aware of our energy.

If you read Muldoon's book, you might notice that he didn't distinguish the etheric from the astral body and etheric and astral projection. J.H. Brennan, in *The Astral Projection Workbook*, started to distinguish the etheric and astral as two different bodies and projection. My experiences confirmed that the etheric body and astral body are two different bodies and it is vital to shift the consciousness from physical to etheric to astral, not directly to astral, it just does not work that way. Although Muldoon and Brennan were different in explaining the difference (and the importance) of each body to promote astral projection, they agreed that working with the etheric body (or the pure energy occupies the same space as the physical body) is important in astral projection.

However, to work with the etheric body, we are required to be able to sense it. The other side of this requirement is that the etheric body must be cultivated. Muldoon and Brennan didn't specifically discuss the etheric body cultivation in their works. Therefore, I do it in this book.

The etheric body is there with you, always. However, as we discussed already, it functions in its default settings. To make it works for any additional tasks like astral projection, it must be cultivated. The cultivation of the etheric body is important to ensure that it does not carry excessive workloads as this will negatively impact the physical body.

In Traditional Chinese Medicine (TCM), it is long known that the physical maladies can be caused by the instability of the etheric body. The most potential factors of the etheric body instability are blocked energy channels (meridians) or stagnation occurred in certain energy centers (dantiens). They, the Chinese healers, used needles (in acupuncture) to "open" the blocked energy stream. I inform you this so you are aware of the importance of etheric body cultivation before trying astral projection.

The physical problem is not the main impact of the etheric body instability. For the sake of our purpose, I must tell you that the instability of the etheric body also affects your psychical experience including astral projection. You might have watched in movies that psychics feel tired after doing a psychic like helping people with their psychic power. Unfortunately, it also happens in the real world. All psychical works require an enormous scale of energy. It requires the energy to flow freely across the energy stream. Without sufficient energy levels, any psychic experience cannot occur. You can think of a light bulb that needs a wire and a battery to on. Either the wire or the battery must work properly for the light bulb to on. It must be the simplest illustration for us.

Fortunately, etheric body cultivation should not be complicated. We can absorb the pure energy to supply the etheric body with additional energy (for an additional task) and distribute the energy across the channels (to unblock the blocked channels). The pure energy is available everywhere especially under shady trees or anywhere around the beach (the seawater contains pure energy). I am not saying that we cannot do the practice indoor because pure energy is everywhere, as long as the room is well-ventilated.

If you are really new to this, you may wonder how the etheric body feels like. Let's pause that for a moment and look at the potential cause of the energy blockage first.

It may be quite surprising that the most potential causes of energy blockage are *overthinking* and *negative emotions*. These don't only block your energy channels but also weaken your energy level. Negative emotions like anger, worry, sadness, doubt, jealousy, and stress (for any reason) will directly impact the etheric body. These negative emotions deplete your pure energy and consequently weaken the etheric body. It is not surprising that constant negativity can cause physical illness besides psychical imbalance. Besides those negativities, the *atmosphere* around us also affects energy. For example, being in the cold temperature room for an extended time can weaken our body because our pure energy works hard to maintain body temperature. This consumes a lot of energy and for that reason, we usually feel weak in the cold atmosphere. The next potential cause is the *lack of quality sleep*. Although it is said that sleep deprivation can trigger OBE, it is unproductive. Sleep deprivation forces the brain to sleep (micro-sleep) and OBE happens. Having good quality sleep is important to recharge the etheric body. The last cause is *food* or what we consume in general. Raw foods are recommended to recharge energy and heavy food (meat) consumes too much energy for digestion. Physical damage, of course, can affect the etheric body as well and we hope that it will never happen to us.

Now, how does the etheric body feels like?

If we pay attention to our etheric part by calming our mind and doing some breathing exercises, we can feel it; individuals may have a different experience with this. The etheric body, usually, feels like smooth electromagnetic impulse or vibration. Some people may feel it warm or cool. Some people may feel tingling. If some people said that they feel nothing, it does not mean that they have no etheric body but they just could not sense it.

Usually, it is easier to sense the energy in the palms because the sensation is stronger in those parts. You might have seen that most people started to practice energy cultivation by making energy-ball between their palms. However, we are required to be able to sense the etheric body overall the body and not in certain parts of the body. Therefore, if you are really new and have no experience in sensing the etheric body, you are lucky. If the energy is stronger (the sensation) in certain parts and weaker in other parts, it can be very annoying. So, being able to sense the etheric body evenly is important and better.

I have provided a simple practice to sense, absorb, and distribute the energy to supply the etheric body with pure energy. You can find the practice in the second part of this book and immediately practice it. It takes time and patience to cultivate the etheric body. Nevertheless, it is recommended to keep reading until this part finished.

While-Projection

One of the reasons why many people failed projecting was this: they didn't obey the "procedures." Do not confuse "procedures" and "techniques." Techniques are anything that we do to execute the procedure or the step in each procedure. Now, let's see the procedures of astral projection.

Physical Relaxation

Astral projection is usually started with physical relaxation. The physical body needs to be in a totally relaxed state for some reason. Firstly, the energy cannot flow freely across the tense muscles. Secondly, the mind usually focuses on the tension (because you feel uncomfortable with that tension); this will hold the energy in that part because the energy flow follows where the mind goes. This leads to double difficulties: the difficulty to sense the etheric body that results in the difficulty to shift the awareness from the physical body to the etheric body, and the difficulty to put the body into sleep-mode.

Tension in the physical body can be generated by physical position or the mind and emotion. It is also important to note the connection between the body and the mind. This connection tells us that any tension in the physical body can influence the mind and the mind processes can influence the body. The point I am trying to make is that we need to detect the original source of the tension.

Certainly, there are many relaxation techniques proposed by experts. However, we need to pick the appropriate technique which is based on the detection of the source of the tension. Picking an inappropriate technique will not give you any result; the tension may be going worse. If you doubt the source of the tension, you can pick the hypnosis technique which I believe the best technique to relax the body and the mind at once.

In hypnosis, relaxation is performed by working at the body, breath, and mind at once. We call that *progressive relaxation*. This technique allows you to systematically "scan" the parts of your body (from head to toes or the reverse) and by using certain imagination you release the tension followed by deep and long exhalation. If you detect any pure physical tension (fatigue) in any parts of the body, you can give a little massage to that part.

I assume that you are lying on your back in the bed. Now, close your eyes and take some nice deep breathing and feel your body. Then, imagine that you are in the most comfortable place (a beach, under the trees in the forest, in a camp, etc.) still in that position. Imagine the wind smoothly blows your face and enjoy the imagination. Breathe deeply and slowly but do not force yourself. It is also recommended to breathe as naturally as you can. As you exhale, use your feeling. Feel your face and head become as relaxed as the wind slowly blows it. Be aware that you are enjoying the place in your mind. Ignore any thoughts popup in your mind (about work, not-working relationship, anger, and so on). Just enjoy it.

Use the same imagination to work with the other parts of your body. Drop your shoulders down and keep the imagination runs. When you reach the toes, wiggle them for a while and imagine the smooth wind blows from your head down to the toes and exhale slowly and fully so that the relaxation can go overall your body.

Be aware that you may fall asleep during this relaxation but there is nothing wrong with that. Don't blame yourself for falling asleep because it is a sign that your body really needs to sleep. This technique takes some times and you should not be hurried in doing this relaxation if you want a good result.

Surely, you can also do this relaxation while sitting on a chair with a back. Just make sure that your elbows and knees are neither too straight nor too bent. Just free them. Wiggling your fingers and toes are important because at the "end-points" of the body they are usually easy to experience fatigue during relaxation.

Physical relaxation must be mastered so that you can enter the relaxed state whenever and wherever you want. It means that you must dedicate your effort to practice it for some time. Relating to that mastery, I suggest you practice progressive relaxation every day especially after work when your physical body really begs of rest. Again, it is fine to fall asleep and never hate that. If you really understand the astral projection, you will be aware that your body really has to sleep for astral projection to occur. So, it is fine to fall asleep. The key is to record into your subconscious mind that whenever and wherever you are in that position (and imagine that thing), you enter an extremely relaxed state. Remember this: extreme physical relaxation is the first condition that initiates the astral projection.

Trance State

Once you entered the total physical relaxation and almost fall asleep but you are still conscious, you are in the trance state. This implies after mastering your physical relaxation technique, make sure that you remain conscious: you are aware that your body is asleep but you are awake. In other words, don't fall asleep.

Perhaps, you are asking this: should I return to the physical place or keep imagining? The best answer is to keep imagining. You cannot imagine anything if you are unconscious, right? Keep enjoying the imagination and the sensation it produces. The chance is you are no longer conscious of your physical environment; you are more aware of your "imaginary" environment. In this phase, it is not surprising that your imagination goes vivid and knowing this helps you to avoid confusion about where you really are at that time.

In the other book of mine (*The Mind-Bending Protocols*), I described the trance state a little longer than in this book. You can check it out for you want to know more about it. I am keeping this book short so I don't go for it deeply.

The trance state is a natural state that we experience every day and night naturally. However, to enter this state deliberately is often tricky. The progressive relaxation that makes you enter this trance state is derived from hypnosis so what you were doing was the first step to hypnotize yourself (self-hypnosis).

Naturally, we experience trance in some conditions: when we are falling asleep, daydreaming, or praying to God. If we are physically relaxed, it needs 10-15 minutes to enter the trance state. The state is signaled by physical relaxation or even catalepsy, a relaxed mind, and a vivid imagination. However, this is just the first level of the trance state. This trance level is not sufficient for astral projection. You must go deeper.

Experiencing trance means you are already shifted from the conscious to the subconscious mind. Shifting to the subconscious mind, or experiencing trance, is important for you in this case because all psychic abilities reside in the subconscious mind. Without being in the trance state, the access to the psychic abilities is unavailable for you.

The trance state is a multileveled subconscious mind state. Here, let's deal with three of them: light trance, medium trance, and deep trance. For astral projection to occur, you must be at least somewhere between the medium and deep trance, or in the deep trance for the best result. You cannot detect at what level you are without knowing the behavior of each trance level. No worries. I briefly outline them as follows.

Light Trance

This is the first level of the trance. Having entered this state, you feel your eyelids are heavier to open but you actually can open it easily if you return your awareness to your physical body. Your overall body also feels heavier or you are extremely "lazy" to move your body. Floating and falling sensation sometimes appear in this state. The most common sign of this trance state is the lucidity of imagination.

Medium Trance

Most people reported that their heartbeats went slower in this state. You may experience spatiotemporal "distortion"; in other words, you may temporarily forget where you are (physically) and when it is. It is the result of the shift of awareness. Since your awareness is shifted from outward to inward, you become more aware of your internal world than the external world. Your imagination becomes more vivid than in the light trance and you may lose the ability to discriminate reality and imagination, so to speak. Actually, you lose nothing but the conscious mind and the subconscious mind behave differently. As you are in the subconscious mind, your perception is altered. Your thinking mind is in rest and your creative mind is in charge. They work differently. From the conscious level, people will say that you lose the ability to discriminate reality and imagination but it is not necessarily the case. Up to this point, hold yourself from concluding that psychic abilities are merely imagination-made. We are not there yet. In this state, your physical sensations are decreased; people refer this to local anesthesia.

Deep Trance

This is the state where all physical sensations are blocked which is very crucial for astral projection to occur. In this state, hallucination (either positive or negative) may be produced and physical movement turns automatic if any. Again, don't prematurely conclude that astral projection is imagination or hallucination. This state is the very edge of the wakefulness and sleep state. This is the edge between the conscious and unconscious states. It implies that if you go deeper, you will fall unconscious, asleep.

Now, the interesting question is how can you deepen your trance state?

Fortunately, the trance state is deepened automatically as long as you don't quit from the light trance and keep enjoying your imagination and avoiding being unconscious. It takes time, of course. However, it does not matter if you enjoy the process. I suggest you to use a going-down elevator or stairs imagination. Suggest yourself that as you go down, either with the elevator or the stairs, you become more relaxed, physically and mentally. If you cannot do them at once, imagining and suggesting, just keep your imagination consistent. Do not jump from one scene to another scene randomly and quickly. Do not analyze anything. Just enjoy and let it go.

Among the range of the trance depth levels, astral projection takes place best somewhere between the medium and deep trance; deep trance is the best if you don't fall asleep. However, the trance alone cannot make you project. The trance state is required to "separate" you from the physical body by blocking the physical sensation to process within your awareness. It is also required to serve you lucidity of imagination that is important for you to create a "doorway".

Remember that in this state your physical sensations are blocked. However, you can sense anything in your imagination. Your etheric body rises to your awareness and your awareness (on the imaginary plane) can sense anything within it. The auditory sense seldom occurs but the visual sensation is lucid. However, do not compare it to the physical sensation. If I can say, it is much like you are using a VR box. So, it is not like you are seeing with your physical eyes directly, at least in my experience.

Doorway Construction

I still remember one of my projections. I was doubtful whether I was dreaming or not. Well, I fell to lucid dreaming. I was aware of the things around me and I knew that I was dreaming. I put my fingers on the wall of a fence. Then, I pushed it with the intention to pass my fingers through the wall. My fingers went inside the wall and that confirmed my question whether I was dreaming or not.

Being sure that I was in a lucid dream, I intentionally created my "door" which is very crucial in astral projection. I failed to create the door because my awareness returned to my physical body. As I returned conscious physically, I felt a strong jerky vibration and heard noises. I opened my eyes and found myself on the bed (my real bed). I saw the bedcover but the motive changed randomly and very quickly. I knew that I was still in the process. I closed my eyes again and let it go. Then, I was "sucked" by energy and when I opened my eyes, just opened it as I did physically (don't be afraid of returning to the physical body!), I found myself in an unfamiliar place. Weirdly, I knew where it was, a place that I wanted to visit because someone that I always wanted to see. I did everything that I knew I must do, and then I returned to my physical body. It was so exhausting.

The doorway is certainly important for conscious astral projection but even if you fail (like me), your intention to project will be executed but you will "land" on an unfamiliar place (if not into the void). The place that I visited was a place "interiorized" by my subconscious mind but the projection has occurred; you will really know that you leave your physical body. The door is important as a tunnel leading you to the place you want to visit, a familiar place. Is it a physical place or just an imaginary place? Neither. You are projecting to the astral plane which is originally a void. What you find is either the interiorization of your memories, expectation or fear or the etheric plane (exteriorization).

Most people want to visit the physical plane with astral projection. It is not the case. If you want to walk among the physical buildings, you must do the etheric projection. Muldoon explained the etheric projection but the term he used was astral projection. Based on my experience, astral projection "throws" you further to the astral plane and you can "step back" to the etheric plane simply by your will.

Different writers have proposed different imagination or visualization to help you exiting from your physical body. The most popular imagination is *climbing the rope.* This technique teaches you to imagine a line of a rope hanging above you (I assume that you are laying on your back) and you reach the rope by your etheric body and start climbing the rope. As you are sure that you are "away" from your physical body (certainly above it), open your eyes and you will see your body under your feet. It is strongly recommended that you take distance (approximately 6 meters) from the physical body before you open your eyes. Surely, this is a pure etheric projection.

I use the term "door" because that is what I want you to imagine. I want you to imagine a door loaded with intention (where it will bring you to); do you remember Doraemon's magical door? That is it. I tell you this because I am using lucid dreaming as the doorway to astral projection. I found it easier and more pleasant than climbing the imaginary rope. However, as the door is created, you don't walk to the door. You will let the door "sucks" you and this can be scary for a beginner. You got to let it go. At this point, I want to emphasize that astral projection is a matter of letting go. It is not something that we actually do. It is something that we experience. That is why it is called the out-of-body experience. We just provide the condition to the experience to occur. This is the straight difference between astral projection and etheric projection.

Other alternatives are available. Besides the door, you can imagine driving a car at a high speed or riding a motorcycle to a place that you want. Unconsciously, as you are driving or riding away, you have been projected from your physical body. Muldoon, Bruce, and Brennan (the top authors in astral projection) agreed that dreaming riding or driving vehicles are a kind of unconscious projection. This time, you are doing it consciously.

The key to this imagination (driving or riding vehicles) is to allow you driven by the vehicles. You will have a sense of flying within the vehicles and as it goes that way, close your eyes and knowing where you are heading to. As the vehicles stop, open your eyes and there you are.

Reentry

Reentering to your physical body is not as complicated as to leave it. What you need to do is just to be aware of what you want. When you intend to return to your physical body, you don't need to imagine you descend to your physical body from nowhere. You will be quickly aware of your physical body with the energy residue rushing within it. Do not be afraid of this because it is normal since your body asleep and you are awake. It will last in one or two minutes. Move your body and know that you are safe.

Post-Projection (realignment)

Wake up from the bed or the chair and stand up. Turn around and move all your body. Squeeze your muscles and then relax. If you feel dizzy, there is nothing to worry about. Sit and close your eyes. Take some nice deep breath and rub all your body. It is possible that you feel hungry, tired, or sleepy. Both astral projection and etheric projection consume an enormous scale of pure energy and you must either have something to eat or sometimes to sleep to recharge it. This is also important to realign your etheric and physical body. Please do not underestimate this case because if your etheric body is not aligned with your physical body, it is not a good thing.

PROBLEMS IN ASTRAL PROJECTION

Someone may spend the night with a cataleptic body on his bed, trying to experience astral projection but eventually grabs a pillow and sleeps with a myriad of disappointments. In fact, he has followed all the procedures he has read from the books or watched from tutorial videos. Waking up in the morning, he wondered if there were still conditions he had not yet fulfilled so that astral projection could occur.

It is still better if he thinks about it. Most people just stick to the procedure but do not realize that there are still other factors that can hinder and even thwart the efforts to get this amazing experience. These people ultimately concluded that the astral projection was just nonsense.

The discussions we had so far should make us aware that astral projection is an experience that involves many factors. While it is true that we unconsciously experience astral projection while natural sleeping, we also know that sleep is an experience that requires several conditions to be fulfilled. How many people have trouble sleeping because their minds are constantly processing information? How many people have difficulty falling asleep because they cannot make themselves comfortable? How many people need medicine to sleep well? The facts show that sleepiness is not the only factor for a person to sleep. If natural sleep alone requires several conditions to occur, how can we assume that astral projection can occur only by following procedures? We even know that natural sleep does not require more procedures except lying down and closing the eyes.

People must understand that astral projection procedures are carried out so that the conditions for astral projection can be fulfilled. However, not all determinants are covered by the procedure. Furthermore, the implementation of the procedure must be accompanied by knowledge of the purpose of the procedure. Thus, people must be able to measure the results of their efforts while carrying out these procedures. To decrease the number of the victims of the failure of astral projection, in this section I will review the problematic factors that usually make a person fail to experience astral projection but they are not aware of it.

Noisy Mind and Insufficient Trance Level

No way! All psychic phenomena occur only when the mind is relaxed or able to focus on an object or idea. If the mind keeps "jumping" around, there is no chance to experience any psychic phenomena including astral projection. Sylvan Muldoon, in his book *The Projection of the Astral Body*, taught that the mind must constantly hold the idea like "I am going to project". Other writers suggested focusing on the breath or any sensation (falling, floating) but the point is to keep the mind focus on an object or idea.

Actually, the mind always focuses on one object at one time. However, the duration of the focus is short and the mind changes its focus randomly. The key to decreasing the noise of the mind is on the practice to endure the duration of focus towards one object.

The mind is noisy in the *beta state*, although we have no problem to think. The mind always thinks and if we don't give it something to think, it will pick anything from the subconscious mind to think; even the thing that we don't want to think at all. The mind will decrease its information processing if it is in a deeper state like *alpha* or *theta* state. That's why it is important to be at a sufficient trance level. One of the purposes is to silent the mind.

There are two main duties of the mind: thinking and imagining. The term noisy mind refers to the two but especially to the first. Being critical to the procedure, questioning what you are doing, thinking of what can happen to you, or remembering what happened in the afternoon, are conditions that sabotage your effort. The worse thing is that the mind never stops "jumping" from one idea or question to other questions or ideas in a high-speed. However, like a normal person, you have the ability to control it. With effort and patience, your mind becomes calm and as you enter the trance it will be calmer. The deeper the trance level, the calmer and more focused the mind will be.

The Condition of the Etheric Body

Experts had different beliefs about the condition of the etheric body required for astral projection to occur. Bruce and Brennan believed that the etheric body must be energized because OBE can be exhausting. Muldoon, on the other side, believed that the stronger the etheric body, the more difficult the astral projection will be. He believed that during sleep the astral body (he meant etheric body) is projected to be recharged. He implied that if the etheric body does not need to be recharged, then the projection does not occur. I agree with Bruce and Brennan because of my experience. Moreover, natural projection and conscious projection are two different experiences. In conscious astral projection, we need to generate etheric sensation over the physical body so that we can control the vibration and this could not happen optimally if the etheric body is weak.

Unstructured Procedure

Certainly, there is no universal technique of astral projection. Many writers or video-makers persuaded their "products" by giving the title like "the most powerful technique of astral projection" or "a 100% working technique of astral projection", while the truth is there is no universal technique that can work for everyone. While the universal technique does not exist, the procedures do.

The procedure contains several steps that must be performed by obeying its sequence. We cannot pick one step and ignore the other steps or randomly execute the steps. In other words, we cannot change the sequence of the steps if we want to have the expected result. However, many people are not patient enough to follow the steps.

Etheric Body Passivity

Imagine a glass of water. Can the water move while the glass is stationary? The water is the etheric body and the glass is the physical body. Usually, if the glass is stationary, the water inside is still. Likewise in the astral projection, the passivity of the physical body will trigger the passivity of the etheric body. However, to experience astral projection, the etheric and astral body must be able to move without making the physical body reacts.

It must be understood that the movement of the physical body is managed by the etheric and astral bodies. On the other side, the movement of the etheric body is managed by will or desire, a feeling of wanting to do something, that Muldoon might call *stress* in his book.

The action to still the physical body (relaxation) is initiated in the mind but when the body has been "incapacitated" to move, the etheric body is free to move, under certain conditions. Most beginners are too afraid to move. They think that if they move, it is the physical body that moves.

The movement of the etheric body is important to make it active or it will be passive as the physical body. We can use imagination, will, and desire to do something to move the etheric body. Try to think of a habit that you always do while in bed. I like to roll to the left and right while in the bed so when I have successfully put my physical body to the sleep-mode, I use my will or desire to roll my body. However, if we are "too conscious" of the physical environment, the chance is the physical body reacts to the attempt.

When you are in the vibrational state, make sure that you are in a deep trance. Then, generate the feeling of wanting to do something like rolling your body in the bed. Since the physical body is incapacitated to move, it cannot respond and the etheric body will respond to the will.

Lack of Imagination

Astral projection, like other psychic phenomena, is initiated in the subconscious mind. Imagination has no direct relationship to astral projection, of course, but it is important. Imagination triggers the subconscious mind where all the psychic abilities reside. In the subconscious mind or trance, we become not "too conscious" or physically alert. Although it is said to keep being conscious while the body asleep, "too conscious" can hold you back to your physical body because you are alerted of the place and things around you, the physical plane. Imagination is important because it leads you to be conscious of the subconscious level and brings you away from "too conscious" to the physical plane.

Fear and Excitement

The feeling of falling or floating or moving, the electrical vibration and the buzzy-noisy sound within the head, and other initial symptoms of astral projection may be scary for beginners. We tend to fear the unknown and as we just begin to start astral projection, we know nothing about it. From here the fear comes. The fear is getting worse as people read somewhere that the silver cord can be broken and they cannot return to their physical body, or the astral entities can occupy their physical body while they are traveling across the planets, and so on. It is all simply untrue.

On the other hand, when the symptoms come, beginners are excited too much and say "Oh yes it is coming... yes, I am projecting now..." then, they come back to their physical body just after that.

Fear and excitement certainly trigger the alertness of the physical plane and the awareness return to the physical body. It is the reason why many people failed in astral projection. In fact, the most important point in both etheric and astral projection is to know that all of these are about to let go. It may be scary or exciting, but let it go. Whatever may happen, let it happen and don't respond to anything. Imagine that you are a parachutist right when you jump out of a plane. Free yourself from emotions without stressing in your mind that nothing will happen.

Warning: if you are suffering any kind of heart disease, don't try astral projection!

Unsupportive Environment and Time

It is strongly recommended that you practice astral projection in a silent place where your physical sensors can take rest from processing external stimuli. Make sure that you are alone in that room and none can disturb you. After some years practicing astral projection, I can try to do it while there are people who are working on home improvement next to my room. I found that it is a noisy mind that made me failed. However, the silence room is the best place ever for astral projection practice.

Timing is also important here. Astral projection is best to be performed when you are not at work; consider practicing it at the weekend. Also, astral projection is not always easy to be experienced in the midnight. Many people try to practice it in the evening while they are too tired or sleepy. If you want to do it at midnight, it is better if you do it at the second cycle of your sleep; sleep for a while and then wake up to practice. It will be easier for your physical body is already relaxed as the result of the previous sleep cycle. My experiences also taught me that early afternoon or morning is good for astral projection especially at the weekend. Find the most comfortable place and time for you.

Part Two

The Etheric Body Cultivation

"In preparing to experience astral projection, we will have to work with the vibration (energy), emotion, and awareness or consciousness."

The etheric body and energy body are synonymous as long as spirituality or mysticism or occultism is concerned. It is the "body" compounded by the pure energy or cosmic energy called *prana*. My study on *mesmerism* several years ago led me to conclude that the *magnetic fluid* mentioned by Franz Anton Mesmer was the etheric body. Mesmer said that the physical and mental imbalance experienced by a human is caused by disharmony between, in my words, the etheric body and the cosmic energy.

Etheric body cultivation can be looked at from two perspectives. Firstly, it can be looked at as certain practices to activate the energy centers in the etheric body called *chakras* or *dantiens* including the practices to overcome the energy blockages in the energy channels called *nadis* or *meridians*. Secondly, it can be looked like a set of practices to build harmony between the etheric body and the cosmic energy or the universe. Energy work systems like Yoga (especially the *Pranayama*) and Qigong are the "blends" of these two perspectives. In fact, it is quite impossible to cultivate the energy body by taking one of them.

In terms of astral projection, the function of the etheric body is emphasized to its role as the intermediary body between the physical body and the astral body. My experiences taught me that the best way to shift the consciousness from the physical body to the astral body is through the etheric body. The etheric body, say, the bridge that makes the consciousness shift possible to happen. Since astral projection requires us to shift the consciousness (or awareness) to the astral body, the role of the etheric body as the intermediary body (or the bridge) is unquestionable. Furthermore, it also makes sense that the etheric body cultivation is a requirement for astral projection to be experienced.

People cultivated their etheric bodies for different purposes. Different purposes require different practices including their difficulty levels and duration. The purpose we are pursuing right now is to prepare the etheric body for astral projection which should not be as difficult as what other people did for their own purposes. The etheric body can play its function without our interference. However, we still need to be able to sense it (clearly and strongly) and it is not difficult (the practices are easy too). Usually, the other writers referred to the state of sensing the etheric body as *the state of vibration*. The etheric body should also be kept strong and healthy because, as Muldoon wrote, the consciousness uses the energy up. Attempting to experience astral projection consumes a lot of energy and energy deficiency can lead to physical maladies. Fortunately, the practices that I outline for you in this part also serve that purpose.

ETHERIC BODY "PLUMBING" SYSTEM

You might know that the pure energy in our body flows just like the air (respiration) and the blood in our physical body. Our physical body has managed the "pipes" for the air to go in from the nostrils and out from the lungs; the blood flows through its channels we call veins. The energy flows through its channels called *meridians* (Qigong term) or *nadis* (Yoga term). The structure of the channels can be imagined as the etheric body "plumbing" system. As a system, it tells the direction of the energy flow. The direction of the energy flow goes to the energy centers (or pure energy storage) called *dantiens* (Qigong term) or *chakras* (Yoga term) and from these centers, it goes to the overall body, transforms into physical energy energizing the parts of the physical body including to maintain the form of the body as we discussed in the first part.

Allow me to use Qigong terms today so we don't have to waste our time just to mention different terms that refer to the same thing.

The meridians and the dantiens are the foci of the etheric body cultivation. Basically, there are thousands of meridians in the human body but talking about the direction of the energy flow we have only two main directions: up and down. If we physically stand on the ground, we have four sides of the physical body: right, left, front, and back. We need to pay attention to the last two sides: front and back. You must remember that when the energy flows up, it goes through the backside and when it flows down, it goes through the front side. So, it really looks like a wheel goes forward; the backside of the wheel goes up and the front side of the wheel goes down. Of course, you can reverse the direction but you don't want it if you know the risk.

After knowing the direction of the flow, we also want to know the point where it starts and the point where it ends. For some reason, the sensible etheric body is supplied by one of the dantiens, the lower dantiens. The energy can flow up from the soles of the feet (the starting point) and down to the toes (the ending point) but it always transits to the lower dantien that we discuss below. Actually, the flow of energy is a never-ending process; it is a circular flowing motion. If it must end at a certain point, it must be either ended in the dantien or the earth.

Now, let us take a look at the dantiens. Please understand that the discussions do not cover all aspects of the dantiens. The only basic overview is presented here.

THE CONSTITUENTS OF THE ETHERIC BODY

Dantiens (or *dantian*) are three energy centers that function as dynamic energy storage in the human etheric body. They are physically associated with some internal organs like intestines, heart, and pineal gland. I prefer to see these organs like the "pointers" to tell us where the dantiens are located. These physical internal organs are not dantiens.

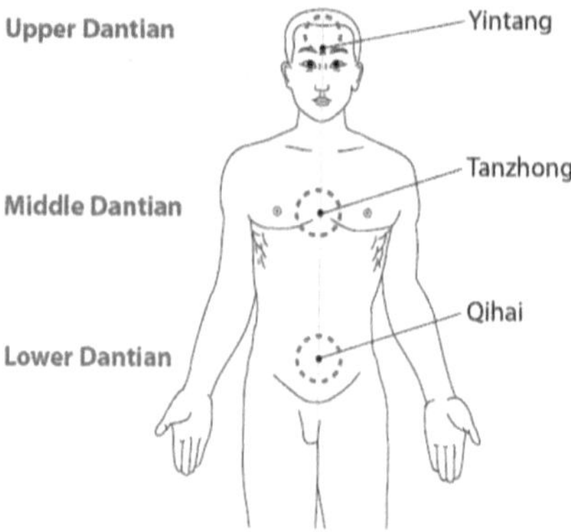

The first dantien is located approximately 5 cm under the navel and 5 cm deeper than the skin. The Chinese name of this dantien is *Qihai* while in English it is known as *Solar Plexus* or *Lower Dantien*. This dantien functions to transform the essential substance that maintains the vitality of the physical body (called *Jing*) to the energy called *Qi*. Energetically, the physical body is supplied by the energy stored in this dantien. When we talk about chi or qi, we refer to the energy of this dantien. The strength and health of the etheric body depend on this dantien. Moreover, it is the energy (qi) in this dantien that is distributed to the overall part of the physical body after transformed from jing to qi. This qi is then sent to the middle dantien to be stored.

The second dantien is located in where the heart is located. Some people said that it is at the center of the chest and some other people said that it is quite to the left of the chest. The Chinese name of this dantien is *Tanzhong* while in English we call it *Middle Dantien* or *Heart Plexus*. The function of this dantien is to store the qi and transform it to *Shen*. The original translation of shen is spirit but we can understand it as consciousness. The middle dantien is closely related to the bio-electromagnetic field emitted from the heart center and reach several inches over the skin. This field is known as the aura. People said that the aura represents the emotional state of you and therefore the middle dantien is responsible for the emotional balance of you. When you have a certain feeling, it feels in the chest. That is where the middle dantien is located. The energy in the middle dantien is transformed to shen and sent to the upper dantien.

The third dantien is located at the center of the brain behind the forehead. This dantien is physically associated with the pineal gland but if we think of shen as the consciousness, this dantien refers to the overall brain. Chinese called it *Yintang* and in English, we call it *Upper Dantien*. For some reason, the same dantien is related to the famous *Third Eye*. When we are thinking about something, we know where the thinking process is taking place. It points the location of the upper dantien; within the head. This tells us that the upper dantien is responsible for mind, awareness, and consciousness.

From the brief description of the dantiens above, the pure energy seems to travel from the lower dantien (jing) to the middle dantien (qi) to the upper dantien (shen). However, it is not exactly the case. The lower dantien is about the power or strength or vitality of both the physical and etheric bodies. The middle dantien is about emotion. The upper dantien is about consciousness. Although we know that the mind influences the emotion and the emotion influences the body (please recall the psychosomatic concept in psychology), but we also know that a physically weak person can have a strong mind (e.g. Stephen Hawking). In other words, these three dantiens can work independently.

These three dantiens are connected by the meridians channel. Thought, it is not wise to bring the energy from one dantien to the other dantien because as the pure energy enters certain dantien, it is transformed into a particular essence that plays a different role in our life. Each dantien is rechargeable directly by practicing certain exercises so we don't generate the energy in the lower dantien and pull it up to the middle dantien; it is not working that way. The energy in the lower dantien, of course, flows to the other parts of the body including the heart and the brain. However, having a healthy brain does not mean someone is smart and having a healthy heart does not mean someone is benevolent. It is what you think affects your upper dantien and it is what you feel that affects the middle dantien. The middle dantien is subtler than the lower dantien and the upper dantien is subtler than the middle dantien, so to speak.

These three dantiens are the constituents of the etheric body that connect the physical body and the astral body. We already know that the consciousness resides in the astral body but it can affect the etheric body and the effect can be manifested in the physical body. The consciousness is "detectable" at the physical level because of the etheric body through the upper dantien. The emotion is manifested in the physical level because of the etheric body through the middle dantien. The strength is manifested in the physical level because of the etheric body through the lower dantien. Up to this point, we should see the different functions of the dantiens and how important they are.

In astral projection, we don't work directly with the dantiens. However, since the etheric body must be cultivated for the best "version" of astral projection to be experienced, we have to work with the dantiens. In preparing to experience astral projection, we will have to work with the vibration (energy), emotion, and awareness or consciousness. Transcending these three elements is the heart of astral projection and other spiritual development. Shifting the consciousness from the physical environment to the astral environment is also possible if bridged by the etheric body. So, the importance of the etheric body (dantiens) cultivation is unquestionable, especially in astral projection.

THE COSMIC ENERGY

The term cosmic energy refers to the pure energy or prana available in the space which is everywhere. This pure energy should not be confused with the energy we study in physics (light, kinetic, thermal, etc.). All physical energy is transformed from pure energy. The prana is the pure energy that transforms into many forms, energy and matters. Many people took a shortcut by assuming that the cosmic energy is oxygen just because both in Qigong and Yoga use breathing to draw in the cosmic energy to the body. However, it is not the case.

Swami Vivekananda, a yogi, wrote in his *Raja Yoga* about this cosmic energy called prana:

> From thought, down to the lowest physical force, everything is but the manifestation of prana. The sum-total of all forces in the universe, mental or physical, when resolved back to its original state, is called prana.

Based on that quotation, I believe that I am not credible enough to explain what it is in a detailed way, none can. I just want to share with you what I know about it (which is very little) and how it connects to the etheric body for its cultivation.

The etheric body is supplied by pure energy either from the food or space; I believe that cosmic energy refers to space.

The cosmic energy is absorbed by the body either consciously or unconsciously. We unconsciously absorb the energy during natural sleep as a default scheduled process takes place in the etheric and astral plane. We are also capable to consciously absorb the energy through mindful-breathing and certain practices we are going to see in this part.

The etheric body interacts with the cosmos through the dantiens that we have discussed above. The dantiens, which are the constituents of the etheric body, functions to draw in the energy and to send the energy out to the universe (e.g. telepathy, energy healing, mesmerism, etc.).

The cosmic energy and air are related. It is true that when we inhale we don't only draw the air but also the pure energy; the Chinese word of the cosmic energy is *ch'i* which can be translated to *air*. However, cosmic energy is neither the air nor the oxygen for we cannot direct the air and the oxygen with the mind but we can do it to the pure energy. The air and the oxygen cannot be sent out through the feet like in energy grounding but with the pure energy, we can.

Although the cosmic energy is available everywhere, it is taught to us that the morning sunlight, the seawater, the grassy ground, and the shady trees in the forest, are the best "providers" of the cosmic energy. Perhaps, it is so because those are rich in negative ions needed by both the physical and etheric bodies.

The cosmic energy is needed to replenish the etheric body. Mindfully, we can absorb it (or allow it to flow into the dantiens) to restore the pure energy in the etheric body which will be then manifested into the physical body. We can also absorb the energy to any part of the etheric body like hands or palms but the best way is to absorb it into the dantiens.

The first requirement to absorb cosmic energy is to know that it exists. The second one is to be sensitive to it; we are required to be able to sense it so we can direct it flows or know where it flows.

The cosmic energy is, of course, etheric. We can only sense it by the etheric body. Fortunately, the etheric body and the physical body is inseparable (except by death) so that what the etheric body sense is sensible to the physical body as long as we shift our awareness to the etheric body.

Sensing the pure energy is relatively easy because we don't have to add anything to us to sense it. We have it every time but we tend to be aware more of the physical dimension of our existence than the etheric dimension. What we need to do is to shift the awareness towards the etheric dimension by doing some easy exercises.

The key to pure energy-sensing is having a relaxed body and mind. The more relaxed you are, the more you able to sense it. Individuals may have different sensations; it may appear as warmth, coolness, vibration, electrical or magnetic impulse, etc. from now on, I use "sensation" to refer to any sensation that you may feel.

Practice A: Sensing the Pure or Cosmic Energy

A1: Take a comfortable position, either standing or sitting. This can take time so you want to have a position that you can stand or sit in an extended time.

A2: Deliberately relax your body from the head to toes.

A3: Close your eyes and breathe nicely for at least 2 minutes. You can set an alarm clock for this.

A4: Pay attention to the "emptiness" of the space around you and know that you are in the unlimited field of pure cosmic energy.

A5: Be aware that *you are energy and your physical body relies on you (as energy)*. This is where you shift your awareness to the etheric body by intention. In this state, you are likely to feel a smooth sensation running across your body.

A6: Raise your hands (while keeping them as relaxed as possible) in the front of you at the chest level or a little bit lower, as if you are going to touch a wall in front of you.

A7: Feel the air or the emptiness of the space that will eventually transform into an energy field that you can sense (remember that the sensation may vary from one to others).

A8: Be aware that nothing is separating your physical body and the energy field. Soon, you will have the sensation over the skin.

A9: Slowly, move your hands in a circular motion and feel the sensation (it is difficult to describe how it feels). The sensation will follow your hands' movement as long as the movement is initiated from your mind. In other words, be mindful!

A10: Put one of your palms to any part of your body (forehead is more preferable) and pay attention to space between them. Soon, you will feel the sensation fills the space. Do the same to the other parts of your body.

A11: Close your practice by putting your palms on your stomach and breathe deeply for some minutes.

A12: Shake your body a little bit to regain your physical awareness.

As you can see that sensing the cosmic energy is relatively easy. However, sensing and absorbing cosmic energy are not alike. To be able to absorb the cosmic energy, you have to permit the energy to enter your energy field. Now, let us turn to the cosmic energy absorption where you will practice to draw in the cosmic energy into your dantiens.

ABSORBING COSMIC ENERGY

The meaning of "absorbing" in this sense is allowing the cosmic energy to enter the dantiens. It is like you open the door and please the energy to freely flow in. The direction of the energy flow depends on your intention. It is strongly recommended to work with the lower dantien at first; it can take time and the longer the better. Please consider working with each dantien on a different day.

As you will see, the instruction is easy and the same for all dantiens with a few modifications. However, one thing you must not ignore before working with each dantien is *grounding*.

Grounding means connecting with the earth both in the physical and etheric levels. The function of grounding is to release "old energy" or negativities (emotions are energy too!) and to avoid energetic overload within you.

Grounding instruction: Either standing or sitting, be aware that you are physically connected to the earth. Bring all your weight down to the bottom of your body that is connected to the earth. Allow the gravitation to pull you down and keep relaxed. Be aware of the pulling force of the earth and allow your energy to go down and merge with the earth. If you are standing, imagine that you are a tree and the root goes down from your soles into the earth. Then, feel that you and the earth are one energetically.

You must start your every practice by grounding your energy that way!

Breathing is important in working with pure energy. It has been long known that inhalation is associated with the pull and exhalation is associated with the release (or push out the energy). Therefore, keep in mind that your intention or mind directs the energy flow and your breathing starts the work.

Instruction B: Filling the Lower Dantien

B1: Find a place that you believe rich in pure energy (forest, beach, or grassy ground).

B2: Find a flat ground for you to stand on so you can keep the balance of your body while standing.

B3: Make sure that you are barefoot and your toes point forward. The knees should not be in a locked position.

B4: Grounding

B5: Activate your sensitivity to the pure energy around you. Put your hands away from your ribs and feel the space between them. Open your fingers and keep your body and mind relaxed.

B6: Close your eyes and mentally "interact" with the energy field by generating the feeling of "I like you" to the energy and the need for it to enter your lower dantien. If needed, beg for it.

B7: Put your palms on your bellybutton; your left palm is under your right palm. This way, you set your intention. You may sense your lower dantien response by one or other ways (warmth, vibration, etc.).

B8: Start inhaling from the nose slowly and deeply. Make sure that you breathe from your stomach, not your chest. Mentally count to 6 when you inhale.

B9: Hold it in your stomach for 4 seconds.

B10: Exhale from the mouth slowly (make your lips like you are blowing a candle) and fully while mentally counting to 6. Do not move your attention away from your lower dantien.

B11: Hold it empty for 4 seconds and start inhaling the same way again.

Note: B8-B11 is called one cycle

Do this practice for at least 10 cycles. After that, be grateful for the universe to give you pure energy. Then, shake your physical body slowly to make it more relaxed. Then, be silent for a moment and feel the energy is "distributed" to the parts of the body that need it the most. Take some days to practice to fill your lower dantien. However, do not imagine that your dantien can be full of energy; the dantien is never full of energy.

Instruction C: Filling the Middle Dantien

C1: Sit comfortably on a chair with a back. Your spine must be straight but don't make it tense.

C2: Relax your body and mind.

C3: Grounding.

C4: Close your eyes and be aware that you are within an energy field.

C5: Shift your attention to your chest (inside it).

C6: Build positive emotions by reminiscing about an enjoyable moment and be grateful for your life.

C7: Place your right palm on the center of the chest and feel your heartbeat.

C8: Beg for the pure energy to flow into your middle dantien.

C9: Inhale deeply while mentally counting to 6. In this practice, you breathe with your chest.

C10: Hold it for 3 seconds.

C11: Exhale fully while counting to 6 and make the sound *haaa*...

C12: Hold it for 3 seconds and repeat the step C9.

Note: C9-C12 is called one cycle.

Do this practice for at least 10 cycles. After that, be grateful for the pure energy and rub your chest circularly for a moment.

Instruction D: Filling the Upper Dantien

This is the last dantien located at the center of the brain. We know that the location of this dantien is also the location where the finest nerves are also located. Therefore, we should be careful about energetic overload in the brain that can ruin your day.

D1: Sit in a comfortable position; semi-lotus is more preferable.

D2: Relax your body and mind.

D3: Grounding.

D4: Put your awareness on the top of your head.

D5: Place your palms beside your head; your fingers touch your brain hemispheres respectively.

D6: Beg for the pure energy to flow into your upper dantien through the top of your head.

D7: Inhale slowly and deeply while paying attention to your upper dantien. You may feel it like filled by the air. As you inhale, mentally count to 6.

D8: Hold it for 3 seconds.

D9: Exhale slowly and fully while pronouncing the sound *mmm...*

D10: Hold it for 3 seconds and repeat the step D7.

D11: Rub your head slowly to make it relaxed and you are done.

Note: D7-D10 is called one cycle.

You should do this practice for at most 10 cycles. Please do not extend it! The sound *mmm...* you make during exhalation is expected to vibrate the upper dantien. This should not be treated as a mantra.

Part Three

Astral Projection Supports

"One of the biggest difficulties in astral projection is separating the etheric and astral bodies from the physical body. One of the biggest mistakes made by beginners is not knowing where they have to go or where they need to be."

W e already know that astral projection is a natural phenomenon because we unconsciously experienced it during natural sleep. This implies that experiencing conscious astral projection requires additional works to support the process. In this part, I outline some useful practices to support your astral projection experience, or experiment.

HYPNAGOGIC STATE (HYPNAGOGIA)

This state has been mentioned and briefly explained in the previous parts. This is a state of mind when you are still awake when your body is trying to sleep. This is an experience of the transitional state between wakefulness and sleep. In this state, we have lucid thoughts or imagination and it is possible to experience sleep paralysis in this state (no panic!). The hypnagogic state is actually pleasant if you are looking for it deliberately.

Reaching this state is important to initiate astral projection. Because the imagination in this state is lucid, the desire to move while the physical body is incapacitated becomes clear. The movement is triggered by imagination. In this phase, imagination should be manifested from a desire to project. Imagination itself can be seen as a manifestation of subconscious desire. When the physical body is incapacitated to respond to the desire to move, the etheric body will respond to it. Without clear desire (or lucid imagination), the etheric body will be cataleptic and consequently, no movement produced.

Hypnagogic state can be induced easily but it surely takes time (please understand that *easily* does not entail *fast*). As with physical relaxation takes time, the hypnagogic state does not come fast; while it is true that physical relaxation is a key to enter this state. Therefore, patience is not optional in following the instruction to induce this state.

One afternoon, I was very tired because I worked since morning. I then headed to an empty room that is usually used for resting. In that room, I slept on my stomach on the carpeted floor. Because there were no pillows in the room, I was forced to use my right hand as a pillow. That position might not be comfortable for many people including me. I closed my eyes but I didn't intend to fall asleep. I only took a short break. I can't really remember how long I was in that position and condition. Suddenly I had a very clear vision. I see a blue sky without clouds. A spark of light similar to a white comet crossed the sky. When I saw the light, I didn't remember that I was in the break room. I was "awakened" by my own voice as if shocked by that very clear vision. It is still clear from my memory that my heart beats fast when I get that vision. At that time, I thought maybe I had a vision of the future. After I read various hypnotism articles, I got information that I had experienced hypnagogia.

If you pay attention, the vision that I got wasn't really something I deliberately imagined. It just appeared. This means that anything that may arise in your mental outlook when you are in hypnagogia can originate from your memories stored deep in the unconscious mind. I remember that view that I had seen in a game; it was a flare that was fired into the sky and slowly fell back to the ground. But in that game, the flare is reddish. My mind must have modified some of the flare's properties to make it look white. Now I can always induce myself to experience hypnagogia which I find very effective for astral projection or lucid dreams.

Sleep position does not seem to be very influential in inducing hypnagogia. Perhaps many people suggest taking a supine position but for me, any position is not important. Even in a physically uncomfortable position, you can experience hypnagogia. If you are familiar with the supine position, then use that position. But don't force yourself to take a position and hold on to that position as if it were a position that you cannot change. It will actually prevent you from experiencing hypnagogia. Therefore, when you are working on a hypnagogic experience, change your position if you really want it. This will also help you to experience astral projection in any position.

Close your eyes because inducing hypnagogia is not the same as daydreaming. Make sure that your body relaxes but after that forget your body. That is, do not care about your body anymore. You intend to rest or sleep for a while and just enjoy your rest time. Don't wait for something or hope something will happen. Don't worry about anything. About 10 minutes later, start imagining as if you were somewhere or watching television. I found a way that for me is very simple but powerful. I imagined as if seeing my reflection in a mirror. But I imagine as if I were someone else who saw me doing something through a mirror. Sometimes I imagine a flashlight that is facing me and that dazzles my view. Not infrequently you will get a random vision that alternates in a relatively fast time. I have noticed that visions usually make you alert so that you get out of that condition. This trick might be useful so you can stay in that condition as long as possible: enjoy it. You must enjoy whatever arises in your mental outlook, whatever it is. Even if you see a snake coming towards you, the snake will not peck you. If you have a phobia of snakes, this is also the most practical way to treat it.

The main idea is that if you close your eyes, relax your body and mind, then within a certain duration, you will experience hypnagogia; as long as you don't fall asleep. This, of course, requires you to stay aware. Your conscious mind must be passive but subconsciously you must actively imagine. This requires time and practice. Therefore, be patient. Hypnagogia is not only important for lucid dreams or astral projections but also for other psychic practices. Instead, this is a basis for developing psychic abilities.

Do this exercise in different places, at different times, and in different positions. You can certainly train yourself to induce hypnagogia in a seated position. But you should not try it in a standing position.

ANCHORING THE PROJECTION POINT

One of the biggest difficulties in astral projection is separating the etheric and astral bodies from the physical body. One of the biggest mistakes made by beginners is not knowing where they have to go or where they need to be. This combination of difficulty and mistake is the perfect cause of the failure of astral projection. Astral projection does not have to always start from "out of the physical body" because the astral body can be somewhere outside the physical body in the blink of an eye. To avoid this difficulty, then I advise you to anchor a point where you will be when you are outside your physical body. If you think that this will only lead you to lucid dreams, you might be mistaken.

The point of projection is a location recorded in your subconscious mind that will direct your astral body to be there. If you do not have a point of projection to aim for, then you will experience astral body stiffness which impacts the physical body. If it occurs, you may feel etheric body vibrations but you will become physically alert and your astral projection fails miserably.

The projection point should be somewhere in your home that is far from your bed. You can choose the living room, kitchen, terrace, or other rooms in your home. Many people prefer it if they wake up in their astral body while above or beside their physical body. Within 6 meters, your astral body will be sucked into your physical body because in that distance the link between these two bodies is very active. Therefore, taking another room as your projection point is very important.

The way to record your projection point is relatively easy even though you have to repeat it several times. Here is how I determine and record my projection point. I choose the living room in my house and I do it at night and day so that I have two sets of memories about that place. This makes it easy for me to experience astral projection both during the day and at night. However, you should start at some time (for example night) as a start.

I went to a corner in the room and stood there for a few minutes. As I stood there, I tried to realize how I felt and what I could observe. Realizing how it feels to be in that place is very important because it will be a trigger to activate the recording in my subconscious mind. Then I moved left and right, turning my body so I could see the other sides of the place. I do this with my eyes open. I touched the wall and recorded how it felt to touch the wall and how I felt about it.

The next step was to close my eyes and realize that I was there; while I was physically there. It is important for me to record all sensations while at that point. I did not pay much attention to the audio sensation in that place. I just need to record kinesthetic and visual sensations. I must be able to feel and realize that I am in that place clearly. Then I returned to silence and realized that I was there.

Just doing it once or twice won't have any effect on your subconscious mind. You have to repeat it several times so that wherever you are you can "call back" the kinesthetic and visual sensations when you are there. Repetition is the key to success in anchoring your projection point.

To find out if your projection point has been recorded in your subconscious mind, try to go somewhere else and lie down or sit relaxed. Close your eyes and concentrate on yourself. Strive so that you can enter hypnagogia.

Sign that you have experienced hypnagogia is the emergence of various mental impressions that are very clear. If you feel this already, try to recall the projection point. You must remember to be in that place, not imagine seeing that place!

If you succeed in "being" in that place, then the projection point is already recorded in your subconscious mind. But sometimes you just stand still in that place and can't look the other way or do anything else. This means you don't record physical activity and physical and mental sensations when you are in that place, or you might do it but it's not recorded properly. You have to repeat it.

When your memory is accessed in hypnagogic conditions, it may be that the recorded impressions undergo certain changes. But the key is you realize that you are in that place.

At the time of the trial, you have not experienced astral projection. You only access projection point recordings. This projection point will not develop during the trial. That is, you cannot go anywhere from this point unless you do it in the context of astral projection.

When you strive to experience astral projection in this way, never imagine that you are going to that place. It will not work. All you have to do is "be there", that's all.

If you have difficulty recording your projection point, then you should sit for a moment to do self-hypnosis. Reread the progressive relaxation section in the previous section. Do that when you are physically at your point of projection and start recording. Do not involve any critical or logical thinking in recording your projection point because it activates your conscious mind. If your conscious mind is active then the possibility of your subconscious mind recording your experience is very small. Don't let the slightest doubt interfere with the process of recording your projection point. You may thank me at any time for teaching you this method.

ARE BINAURAL BEATS HELPFUL IN ASTRAL PROJECTION?

I know that people provide binaural beats as an astral projection aid. I have also tried it many times. Do binaural beats really work? Binaural beats are indeed formulated to make us relaxed and in some conditions also trigger etheric vibrations. However, binaural beats do not make you experience astral projection.

In order to experience astral projection, all stimuli originating from the physical senses must be blocked and listening to binaural beats seems to be contrary to astral projection instructions. Binaural beats are very good if used to induce hypnagogia but will not go further than that.

I do not recommend using binaural beats for astral projections because for me it will only waste your time and energy. Furthermore, you never really know if the person who makes the binaural beats understands what he made. Do you think all the binaural beats that are spread on the internet are made by experts? Many people try binaural beats and end up with tinnitus and insomnia. In short, binaural beats are not needed in astral projection. You also don't need binaural beats to experience hypnagogia.

You can fall asleep with binaural beats because you don't have to be awake when your physical body is asleep as needed in astral projection. In astral projection, you must remain conscious (subconsciously) and binaural beats keep you attached to your physical sense of hearing, your ears. This is really annoying if you really realize it.

You may meditate with binaural beats even though you know that the ascetics must go to the slopes of the mountains, the middle of the forest, or the desert so that they are not disturbed by voices. Likewise, astral projection, consciously distracting yourself with irregular sounds (and it is not even clear who made them) is a step back from astral projection.

Monks use sounds such as gongs or sounding bowls to fasten their conscious thoughts; so they don't think about anything other than the sound. When their conscious mind "loses" the bond with the sound, there is nothing left to think about. Therefore, what is used by the monks cannot be compared to what is promised by binaural beats or their makers.

If you read other books about astral projection, you certainly don't find any instructions for using binaural beats. Unfortunately, they also do not explain that binaural beats are completely unproductive in the context of astral projection. Therefore, if you have been using binaural beats to experience astral projection (and certainly fail), then it's time to save all of that and start all over again without binaural beats.

PHYSICAL RELAXATION ACCELERATOR

It is easier to gain physical relaxation if it really needs to take a break. If you noticed my story about the while flare, I was so tired. When the physical body is tired (no need to be extremely tired), it will send signals to awareness like fatigue or just tiredness. You can see that tired people are easy to fall asleep; they are so because as their head touches the pillow, they become very relaxed. The subconscious mind knows that pillows are associated with sleep and the body only knows sleep as a total physical relaxation; please notice that hypnotists often use the command "sleep" to put their clients into physical relaxation.

There are two ways to accelerate the physical relaxation for astral projection. Firstly, you can attempt to experience astral projection at the second cycle of your sleep (sleep for a moment, wake up for astral projection); secondly, you can do some physical exercises just before you put your back on the bed for astral projection.

By "accelerator" I mean the second way. Do some push-ups or karate or whatever you usually do but do not force yourself. Too much tiredness can make it difficult to relax unless you have someone to give you relaxing massages.

It was in the morning. After doing some physical exercises, I got my towel and went to the bathroom. However, there was no enough water in the basin so I must wait for some minutes while tapping it. I went to the bed with a towel around my stomach. I was lying on my back and suddenly I felt my body vibrated. It was so fast that I found myself behind my house for one or two seconds. The combination between my physical tiredness and sleepiness made me fall asleep very quickly; however, because I was waiting for the water and I remember that it was Monday (I must go to work), I was conscious (subconsciously). I believe that it was the reason I experienced "spontaneous" projection.

NO COFFEE IN THE EVENING

It's no secret that a glass of strong coffee can keep us up all night. Meanwhile, drowsiness is one important factor so that astral projection can be experienced. This means you should avoid coffee when you are going for an astral projection; like it or not, they both are enemies of one another.

I do not really understand the effects of caffeine on our bodies but many people experience certain things after drinking a glass of coffee (or two glasses), including me. The loss of drowsiness is one of the effects of caffeine. Maybe this has something to do with coffee breaks that are always done at the beginning of seminars or conferences so that attendees can be awake throughout the seminar time. Some people claim that coffee does not affect the quality of their sleep but most claim the opposite.

Another effect of coffee or caffeine is an increase in heart rate. This seems if I am not overdoing it, quite dangerous for those who have a weak heart. I have already said in other parts of this book that people who have weak hearts should not try astral projection because it can result in death. Things can get worse if someone with a weak heart tries astral projection after drinking a glass of coffee.

Based on experience, as the etheric body accumulates, the heart rate increases and we are more likely to be awake or physically alert. This is caused by the strange sensations we feel in certain parts of our body coupled with the loss of drowsiness needed so that our conscious mind can "fall asleep".

When I started experiencing hypnagogia and I deliberately looked the other way in hypnagogia, my heart felt like it stopped for a moment. This is a pretty terrible experience if I have a weak heart. A person may experience heart failure if the etheric body is slow to trigger the heartbeat to work again.

The effects of caffeine can make matters worse and this is why many people worry about the experience of astral projection. Therefore, I strongly recommend that you postpone the desire to enjoy coffee at night (if you want to experience astral projection at night).

I once drank a glass of coffee during the day and another glass in the evening. After that, on the same night, I made an astral projection and ended up with a racing heart and chest pain that lasted for almost two days. My eyes could not be closed at all and I was in a state of confusion all night.

You certainly don't need to experience the same thing. I don't care how much you are addicted to caffeine; you must be able to refrain from a delicious glass of coffee to experience the miraculous astral projection.

TIMING

Beginners really like to try the experience of astral projection at night. Although there is nothing wrong with that, they should try it in the morning or in the afternoon.

If you are not working one day, then try astral projection in the morning as long as the atmosphere around you is supportive. Get up in the morning and do some physical exercise. After that, get your breakfast but don't eat too much. After that, go wash your body with cool water. You will most likely become very sleepy and this is a good time to experience astral projection.

The afternoon is also a pretty tiring time for most people. Returning from work, we tend to choose to lay our bodies to rest. This is also a good time to try the astral projection experience.

The night is a natural time to sleep but at that time our minds are busy thinking about two things: what happened that day and what might happen tomorrow. When we are trying to sleep, our conscious mind continues to work to process the memories and hopes that are in our minds. Suddenly we fell asleep and woke up the next day.

Having a planned astral projection at night is certainly possible. However, astral projection can be experienced at any time. We just need to be observant in seeing our physical and mental state at a certain time.

There is no prohibition to experience astral projection at night. But try to experience it in the morning and evening. You will be surprised at the results you can get. Of course, make sure that you get support from your physical environment. Light and sound conditions greatly influence the experience so you might need to make some adjustments to get the best results.

NORTH-SOUTH POLES AND GRAVITY

I once listened to a spiritual discourse related to meditation. At that time, the lecturer said that the direction of our body also determines the experience of meditation. He said that it was very important to face the north during meditation. I think this might be related to harmony between the magnetic field of the body and the earth.

Some of my astral projection experiences are related to the north and south poles. I checked for a moment on the compass attached to my cellphone and then adjusted the position of the mattress in my room. I did several experiments with the position of my head and legs.

I tried to put my head in the north position and my feet in the south position. When I experience hypnagogia, I feel there is a pull of energy in my back (I sleep facing west). Several times, I experienced my etheric body turning so that my head was in the east and my feet were in the west. These are my initial experiences and I didn't open my eyes because I didn't know what to do at the time.

Another time, I positioned my head to the south and my feet pointing north. I guess that is of no use. I assume that body position does not affect the experience of astral projection.

What I have found is the importance of keeping a distance between the body and the earth. When I am on a bed about 50 cm from the ground, I get an experience of astral projection more easily than sleeping on a floor on a mattress. I believe that we should keep our distance from being too close to the ground when trying astral or etheric projections. I cannot explain it but I believe that it has to do with gravity.

If you then assume that people who live in high rise buildings experience easier astral projections, then I might agree with you. What's more important is that you get your own experience.

Part Four

The Procedure of Astral Projection

"Astral projection is something that is easy or simple because it is an experience. What is difficult is making us eligible to experience it."

ASTRAL PROJECTION AS EXPERIENCE

One classic tendency is the assumption that astral projection is an action or something we can do. This is a misunderstanding of the phenomenon of astral projection. Actually, astral projection is an experience; therefore it is called OBE.

Astral projection cannot be done but can be experienced. We may fail to experience astral projection but that does not mean we can successfully make an astral projection. Because astral projection is an experience, what we can do is condition ourselves so that the experience can occur.

Astral projection is like sleeping and dreaming. We might be able to do things that can cause the phenomena of sleep and dreams to be experienced but sleep and dreams are not actions. For example, we might try to sleep but we cannot sleep because certain conditions do not qualify for the sleep experience to occur. Meanwhile, some people may try not to fall asleep while working but because they are tired and sleepy they end up on their desks.

We can also try to intend to be able to dream of an ex-girlfriend while we sleep but instead we have nightmares. Even lucid dreams are experiences and all we can do is prepare ourselves so that we are qualified to experience them. This also applies to astral projections.

I say this because many people think that astral projection is something that can be done. The right sentence for this is: the experience of astral projection can be attempted. I really want to emphasize that any astral projection technique that is scattered on the internet (including this book) does not teach us to do astral projection; because astral projection is an experience. That is something we get and not something we do. Such books only teach us how we can experience astral projection.

You have just read a number of things that can support the experience of astral projection. There are still many other things that can support or even reduce the opportunity to experience astral projection and all that you can get at other sources.

Some people who claim to be able to make astral projections consciously do not intend to state that they can do so under any circumstances. They intend to state that they know how they can experience conscious astral projection. In conditions that do not allow them to experience it, they honestly cannot do it either.

I have a number of experiences of conscious astral projection but in some conditions, I cannot experience them either. I really know under what conditions I can experience it and under what conditions I will not experience it. Muldoon is a projector but he himself said (in his book) that conscious astral projection is a rare thing.

The reason why I emphasize this point in this section is so that you can be observant in seeing the possibilities that might interfere with your astral projection experience. In this section, you will also be presented with astral projection procedures that you can test on various occasions.

Keep in mind that I don't offer techniques in this section or in this book. I explain the procedure that underlies the experience of astral projection. Various astral projection techniques are the embodiment of these procedures. Knowing this will greatly help you to experience astral projection. There are hundreds of astral projection techniques but there is only one set of procedures that underlies all existing techniques. This is the same as saying that there are only two sexes, male and female, but there are billions of people's names.

Astral projection becomes very difficult to experience when someone thinks that he has to jump from one technique to another in order to experience it. If he knows that there is only one set of procedures behind the experience of astral projection (which he unconsciously experiences every time he sleeps), then he will realize that actually astral projection is something that is easy or simple because it is an experience. What is difficult is making us eligible to experience it.

Note that we always feel full after we eat as long as we eat a filling meal. Satiety is an experience and eating is a set of procedures that allows us to experience satiety. If we only eat bread and eggs, it is very likely that we will not feel full. Here is the function of the technique. For example, one of the conditions that we can experience astral projection is extreme physical relaxation. If what we do is limited to stretching our muscles then we will not reach a state of extreme relaxation. There are many relaxation techniques that we can use and some techniques only promise ordinary relaxation that does not qualify for an astral projection experience. Likewise with imagination; there are many ways to imagine but not all ways promise a clear imagination that can support the experience of astral projection. Therefore, I do not mean to say that technique is not important.

In this section, I write techniques that can be used to carry out astral projection procedures. I try my best to be able to present the techniques that I think are the best in general. However, once again, there is no technique that can promise the experience of astral projection as long as certain conditions do not qualify. I believe that we have discussed this before.

THE PROCEDURE OF ASTRAL PROJECTION

Apart from the various conditions that can directly influence your astral projection experience, this is a set of processes that occur when someone experiences astral projection.

The Physical Body Falls Asleep and the Mind is Awake

For some people, the statement that our bodies sleep and our minds are awake is nonsense. They reasoned that whatever is experienced by the body is regulated by the mind. If the body is asleep then the mind must be asleep. We must tolerate people who hold such narrow views. This narrow-mindedness forces them to interpret sleep paralysis as the arrival of spirits that oppress their bodies. Of course with this narrow understanding, they also cannot explain how dreams occur.

Maybe some of the mistakes are on our side because of using the term "sleep" on the body because basically the body never sleeps. When we sleep, our bodies continue to work like digesting food, pumping blood, breathing oxygen, releasing carbon, and also replenishing pure energy. Therefore, on this occasion let us align our view of this "sleeping body".

I am forced to use the term "sleep" because it has become a convention in psychic discourse especially when it comes to lucid dreams and astral projections. This is similar to the term hypnosis which should be replaced by *monoideaism*. James Braid intends to replace the term hypnosis with *monoideaism* when he realizes that the term hypnosis is not appropriate to describe the hypnotic state. We still use the term hypnosis today because James Braid was late in changing it.

What meant by the term "sleep" in the body is a condition of very deep physical relaxation. This extreme relaxation condition causes the physical body to become unresponsive. When our physical body sleeps, the connection between mind and the physical body becomes "broken" and therefore the stimuli sent to the brain are not processed and their sensations become undetected. But this condition is a two-way condition. Not only physical stimuli that are not processed in the mind but also mental impulses that are processed in the mind cannot be executed by the physical body. If the physical body does not have the capacity to execute the mind's commands, then those commands will be taken over by the finer body, the etheric body.

The way to "put to sleep" the physical body may be difficult if the conscious mind is still processing various physical sensations. Therefore, physical body relaxation is not enough if only relying on stretching the muscles. The subconscious mind must carry out its creative function to arouse the imagination so that the conscious mind is no longer busy detecting stimuli transmitted by muscles and skin. If consciousness is filled with imagination, virtual sensations will become real and physical sensations will fade from consciousness. This is why the best technique that can be used to "put the body to sleep" is the progressive relaxation technique that we have discussed in another part of this book.

Then, the term "mind awake" refers to our awareness: that we are aware of what we are experiencing. We even realize that our bodies have fallen asleep. There is no way we can imagine if our minds go along to sleep with our physical bodies. Therefore, we don't need to think about what is meant by "mind awake" and how we keep our mind awake. Enough to actively imagine your mind will remain awake. Furthermore, what is meant by "mind" in this context is not conscious thought. It is our unconscious mind that is awake. I really want to say that our conscious mind sleeps with our physical bodies but that will open up a new subject and I do not expect this book to be thicker than it should be.

Progressive relaxation techniques can be combined with physical movement techniques as I have suggested before. We can achieve deep or extreme physical relaxation more quickly (and more easily) if our body feels tired. In a state of exhaustion, the subconscious mind will send relaxation signals to the body without our asking. When combined with progressive relaxation techniques that involve active imagination, we seem to agree with our subconscious mind to put our physical bodies to sleep. This is a collaboration that is very rarely done by many people in order to experience astral projection.

I know that I have reviewed progressive relaxation techniques in the first part of this book. But I will review it again by adding some details so that you are really ready to practice it.

The main idea of progressive relaxation is to consciously relax the physical body from head to toes or from the opposite direction. The subconscious mind also actively works to support the conscious mind in relaxing the physical body because it may be physical muscle tension caused by mental tension. This is the progressive relaxation technique adopted from hypnosis:

Try to start the relaxation process by doing some physical movements such as push-ups, kicking, hitting, jumping, and so on. The aim is to expedite the flow of blood and relax the muscles. After a few minutes doing that, lay your body on the bed. I have to tell you that you don't need to go all out to exercise because your sweat will interfere with further activities.

Now, I assume that you are sleeping on your back on your bed and there is a pillow that is not too high under your head. You must be really comfortable with your current body position.

If you pay attention to the sensation that you are feeling right now, it is a sensation of relaxation. If you feel there is tension stored in certain body parts, massage the part because it might be less moving when you do physical exercise before.

However, you must feel that there is fatigue filling your physical body right now. If that's true, then it's time you close your eyes and start the relaxation process. Let's start from your toes (in the previous section I explained this technique from the head. This time we take the opposite direction).

Imagine that your body is a long and spacious office. Inside the office, there are many people who work in different rooms. Every room has an exit. Your feet are a workspace filled with tired workers. They ask you, as the head of the office, to ring the bell for them as a sign of rest.

Breathe in deeply and gently because the blood needs oxygen to relax your muscles. When you exhale fully, imagine that the exits of your foot room are open and the workers immediately leave the room while turning off the lights in the room. Instantly, the room went dark and there was no movement because all the workers had left the room.

You can imagine the boundaries of the room for example from the tip of the toe to the ankle, knee, or thigh. One thing is certain; the exit must be at the tip of your toe.

After that, you switch to another room, for example from your groin to your stomach. In your imagination, look at workers who are tired and in need of rest. You then ring the bell in the room and the exits (on the sides of your body) open. The workers immediately left the room and turned off all the lights so the room went dark. Don't forget to breathe deeply and gently.

You move on to another room from your chest (don't forget your back) to the base of your throat. This room has two wings namely your right-hand room and your left hand. This is a fairly long room and all the exits are at the tips of your fingers. The workers here seem to be still busy with their work, but you want to remind that the time for rest has arrived. You then ring the bell and the exits open. Immediately the workers left the room from both the right and left side of the room while turning off the lights in the room except for a lamp in the middle of the room. This is your heart that must keep working.

You then check if there are still workers in the throat room to the head. This room consists of several smaller rooms namely the eyes and ears. You get some workers still in the room. You then ring the bell so that the exit located at the tip of your head opens and the workers leave the room, turning off the lights in the room except for a lamp in the middle of the room. That is your room; awareness.

Let's continue with your imagination to take you deeper into the trance state.

Your office turns out to be above a field and below that field; there is a large and deep room. That is the room where the office will be stored; imagine Batman's basement.

Through a computer in your room, you make the office slide down. The more the office went down into the ground, the more invisible the office was; it entered the underground darkness so that it was no longer visible. The further you bring your body down, the more you feel the sensation of "falling" and the deeper trance state will be reached.

Now, only you are in your room. There is a door in your room. The door takes you to another room outside the office. That is the room you do to watch your favorite shows. Or, it is a room that frees you to do whatever you want.

Imagine that you stand up and leave your desk and head for that door. With full confidence, you open the door and enter it. Whatever is behind the door is always in accordance with your own imagination. Don't worry if you forget to turn off the lights in your room because the button is behind that door. You can only turn off the lights in your office (your body, your logical awareness room) from your imagination room. Enter the imagination room and press the button behind the door and know that your office is now safely stored. I say that but actually, at this point, you are no longer experiencing physical awareness.

There are many other progressive relaxation techniques and this is just one of them. If you really mean it and enjoy the process I said above, then you will definitely succeed in "putting your body to sleep" while remaining conscious in your subconscious mind.

This is a hypnagogic state in which all imagination seems clear. For the subconscious mind, imagination is reality and indeed that is the truth. Physical condition is the reality of the conscious mind and imagination is the reality of the subconscious mind. We don't need to make comparisons between these two realities to assume that the imagination looks so real when that's the reality for our subconscious mind.

The Transition of Mind from Gross to Subtler Planes

When you decide to go to another room outside your office, that's when you experience the transition of consciousness from the rough dimension to the finer dimension. However, projections do not occur in this state.

What I mean by the finer dimensions is the etheric body because the etheric body is a finer body right after the physical body. When your consciousness has shifted to the etheric body, you must realize that you are the etheric body itself. If the memory of your physical body returns (and this is very likely to happen), then you must still realize that you are an etheric body while your physical body depends on you as an etheric body. To maintain the continuity of your etheric awareness, you must remain in a state of hypnagogia. The trick is very easy: don't stop imagining and enjoying all the sensations.

Now, I will teach you the most effective way to trigger etheric body vibrations. You just need not be afraid in this way because there really isn't anything to fear. If you have a complaint with your heart, then I already suggest you not to try the experience of astral projection.

In a hypnagogic condition, I met two policemen who each held an electric shock. They walked towards me and when they reached the closest distance they immediately fired a wire that was electrified. It made my body tremble pretty hard and I experienced projection. But this time I did not teach you to imagine being electrocuted by two policemen.

You need to be reminded that in your imagination you should be able to see yourself directly and not through a mirror reflection. That is, you must be able to see and feel your body and in hypnagogic conditions, it does occur. I don't want you to be a ghost in your imagination: a ghost that cannot be seen.

Your imagination must allow you to carry out etheric bodily activities. Activities such as walking, holding, standing, and sitting, must be done with your body in the imagination. You will still remember when I taught to anchor a projection point. I teach you not to imagine seeing that point but being there.

In deep trance conditions, you will indeed feel the sensation like experiencing it physically. If you can only imagine seeing it, that's a sign that you are not in a deep trance.

You will still remember the explanation of sensations that are in the area of consciousness and not the area of the conscious mind. Awareness is in your astral body. When you are in the etheric body, your astral awareness also follows there. It's just that at that time the etheric awareness is more dominating your existence or your awareness. For the dominance of the etheric body to be achieved, you must be able to experience the etheric body vibration which is popularly called the "vibrational phase" in various astral projection books.

So that the continuity of your imagination is maintained, I will use your imagination as a starting point. You still remember that you are now in your imagination room, right? Here's what you need to do while in the room:

In principle, you still use imagination techniques. You can imagine anything as long as that imagination can trigger vibrations in your etheric body.

Electric shock is a common experience that is usually experienced by almost all adults. We could be electrocuted accidentally or on purpose. This time, try to imagine a blue ball of energy. The energy ball is on your desk and you are looking at it.

Make sure that you are aware of what will "happen" to your body if you touch the energy ball. In this case, because it is an energy ball, then when you touch the ball with your palms, the energy from the ball will flow into your etheric body. Energy flowing into your body will vibrate all parts of your body (etheric body) and produce electrical noises.

If when you touch the ball no vibrational sensations appear, that means your imagination or intent is unclear. You must have a strong and clear will in order to create an effect in your imagination.

The vibrations that appear may be soft and slow but you can always increase the intensity with the power of your will. You don't need to worry if the electric vibrations can harm you. This is a safe way to trigger etheric body vibrations.

You also don't have to stop with the imagination I demonstrated. You can change your imagination but you should plan it well in advance. When you are in the space of imagination, you must not "wake up" your conscious mind by asking "what should I imagine" because it will get you out of the trance.

Therefore, before you begin the process of progressive relaxation, you have to imagine energy balls, policemen with electroshock weapons, or being on a moving train. Do not change the contents of your imagination when you are in the imagination space. The imagination space itself contains a lot of random imaginations that originate from your subconscious mind. The doubts that you experience in this situation will only make the condition of your creative awareness even worse.

If you feel a strong vibration, this means that the dominance of the etheric body has been achieved. The dominance of the etheric body is one of the fundamental conditions that must be experienced by a person if he wants to experience projections, both etheric projections, and astral projections.

The Dominance of the Etheric Body

The dominance of the etheric body is a stage when your consciousness has switched from the physical body to the etheric body. You may still feel physical sensations but they are overwritten by etheric sensations. A full transition of consciousness occurs when you really lose physical sensations, but you don't need to check whether you can still feel your physical body.

Your etheric body has the exact same shape as your physical body. Every cell in your physical body has an etheric partner. Therefore, you will feel etheric vibrations as if your physical body were vibrating. Many people think that they are still in the physical body at this stage. They have actually turned to the etheric body but because the etheric body and physical body occupy the same space, this confusion might arise. Beginners usually check at this stage to find out if they can still move their physical bodies. This is a serious error in astral projection. This check will only end in the return of their consciousness to the physical body.

The vibrations of the etheric body (the etheric body indeed always vibrate!) Which is accompanied by a loud electric noise should take our consciousness. In other words, as awareness, we have entered "an etheric vehicle".

Here we find two intersections: whether we will experience etheric projections or astral projections. By using the method of "climbing a rope" or "projection point", we will experience etheric projection. If we use the "door" or "free escape" method then we will go to the astral dimension or experience astral projection.

That is, if we want to experience astral projection, then we still have to move from etheric consciousness to astral consciousness. From this astral awareness, we can experience astral projection.

The Transition of Consciousness from the Etheric to the Astral Plane

This book was written to simplify astral projections and not etheric projections. Therefore I will continue the discussion to the astral dimension.

Strong etheric vibrations are the end of conscious imagination. When we reach this stage, all we have to do is surrender. Don't think that etheric vibration has no direction. The etheric vibration always leads out of the physical body or into the astral body.

My projection experiences taught me that even if our consciousness shifts from etheric consciousness to astral consciousness, the sensation of leaving the body will still be felt. Here, many people assume that the astral projection and the etheric projection are the same. Of course, reality is not the case.

In order to experience the transition from etheric consciousness to astral consciousness, we are resigned to where the etheric vibrations will lead us. The sensation that we will feel is a sensation like being pulled from our spine, our legs, or our chest. Just follow with resignation like a parachutist jumped from his plane.

Let the energy carry you out of your physical body. You may realize that you have left your physical body and you should not open your eyes if you are still close to your body (in your estimation).

The sensation of falling or being pulled that you feel is certainly quite strong and there is no point in you holding on to your physical body. After all, that is not your goal. Your goal is to experience projection, right?

The astral plane is a void or at least that is the safest way to describe it. When you have fully switched consciousness to astral consciousness, you no longer feel the etheric vibration or listen to any sound. You will be floating in a vacuum without a body (not the physical body, not the astral body). But you realize that you are observing the void and you are aware that you are moving.

The movements tend to be slow and if you feel this then you can open your eyes; open your eyes like open your physical eyes.

At this point, you no longer imagine. All forms of changes that occur in the astral plane are in accordance with your will. If you do not get a void, then your consciousness has modified the environment with your memories or your hopes and dreams.

The most important thing you should do when experiencing etheric vibrations is not to panic. You must remain calm and surrender.

Astral Beings

The vibrational phase that I discuss in this book is different from the vibrational phase discussed in other astral projection books. In another book, etheric body vibrations are generated by scanning the physical body. This method is actually good but it still involves the conscious mind. There is one drawback in this scanning method: we still have awareness of the physical body. This will make it easier for us to return to the physical body.

The method I use involves the subconscious mind so that when the etheric vibrations are generated, our conscious mind is ready for sleep. The surrender that I teach you is a farewell to your conscious mind.

That is the core procedure of astral projection, which is resignation. If you are still "too conscious" then you will fail to experience projection.

Astral projection is a transition from conscious consciousness to pure consciousness. Pure consciousness is formless but can be formed using the power of will. That is, when we are in the astral realm, we can "create" a "body" if we want to.

The physical environment in which our body is located is completely gone from the radar of our consciousness; we don't even remember it at all.

Then, where is our etheric body?

Our etheric body has ushered us into the astral body or pure consciousness. Like we deliver a guest, we leave the house for a moment. When the etheric body actually leaves the physical body, our heartbeat stops literally. Then, the etheric body returns to the physical body but there is an unbroken connection of energy to the astral body.

This energy connection still exists to maintain the continuity of the physical body and astral awareness. Without this energy connection, there will be one of two possibilities: we will return to the physical body and leave the "artificial astral body" that we make while in the astral plane or we will experience death. But that is only theory. In fact, the energy connection between the physical body and the etheric body, the etheric body, and the astral body, will never break.

The existence of this energy connection causes the transfer of consciousness to occur. Even though the etheric body still occupies the physical body, a small part of your consciousness still manages it. But most of your awareness is already in the astral plane. Robert Bruce calls this phenomenon "mind-split".

This energy connection also causes the transfer of memories. Without this energy connection, our astral projection experience cannot be recorded in our physical brain. Furthermore, this energy connection allows us to return whenever we want and also allows us to detect the signals sent by our physical body.

Thus, you don't need to worry about astral projection. You still have control over your physical body and your etheric body. Some of your consciousness still exists in the physical and etheric body. We are only truly cut off from these two bodies if we die.

Many people report their experiences of meeting astral beings. These creatures are projections of our own consciousness. If we are worried about meeting demons in the astral realm, actually these demons are in this physical realm as well. We are not aware that there are many spirits around us. There is no need to go to the astral realm to meet these creatures. If we meet with astral beings, it means these creatures have entered our field of consciousness all this time.

These creatures incarnate into all the negativity that we keep, such as revenge, jealousy, malice, anger, hatred, and so on. All forms of negativity that lead us to bad deeds are Satanic. The astral realm, for the last time, is a void. It is our consciousness that gives it shape.